Valerie Laws and Richard Wall

MARY GLASGOW PUBLICATIONS

Introduction

Au secours has been written to introduce you to the most important words and phrases you will need if you visit a French-speaking country, or if you meet a French person in your own country. These should give you the confidence to manage most situations in which you are likely to find yourself.

Au secours is different from most language books: each unit is self-contained. There is no need to work your way from the front of the book to the back – you can study the units in any order you like. The words you need are set out clearly at the beginning of each unit, as shown in the example below, and you should not need to know more than a very few words from other units.

▶ **Words you will need:**

bonjour	hello, good morning, good day, good afternoon
allô	hello (only on the telephone)

All the instructions are in English. Your tutor or teacher may choose to say the instructions in French, but if you get confused you will be able to check in the book to understand what you are supposed to be doing! If you need help with a word or a phrase, you can always look back to the word list at the beginning of that unit.

Au secours is different in another way as well. It teaches you French without asking you to learn too many rules of grammar. You'll find that you can get by with very little.

As you work through the tasks, remember they are all designed with one thing in mind: to help you to understand and use the key words and phrases as quickly and easily as possible. As you finish each unit, think back over what you have been doing, and then fill in your record sheet.

GOOD LUCK!

Contents

Introduction
1. Saying hello and goodbye 2
2. Numbers and prices: 1–69 6
3. At the post office 10
4. At the restaurant 14
5. At the campsite 18
6. Train travel 22
7. At the bank 26
8. The weather 30
9. Asking the way 34
10. Café and snack bar 38
11. At the tourist information office 42
12. At the petrol station 46
13. Meeting people from other countries 50
14. Breakfast 54
15. Hiring something 58
16. Going by bus 62
17. Lost property 66
18. Telling the time 70
19. Booking at a hotel 74
20. On the métro in Paris 78
21. Feeling ill 82
22. Dinner at a restaurant 86
23. Filling in forms 90
24. Numbers and prices: 70–100 94
25. Directions 98
26. Buying bread and cakes 102
27. Accident or emergency 106
28. Likes and dislikes 110
29. Making friends on holiday 114
30. Buying fruit 118
31. When your car breaks down 122
32. Taking notice 126
33. Colours and sizes 130
34. At the chemist's 134
35. Arranging a meeting 138

▶1◀ Saying hello and goodbye

You can probably manage without this unit! But you will feel much more at home if you can say and understand all these things, and people are likely to be more friendly towards you.

▶ **Words you will need:**

bonjour	hello, good morning, good day, good afternoon	*madame*	madam	(The French use these much more often than we do)
		monsieur	sir	
		mademoiselle	miss	
allô	hello (only on the telephone)			
bonsoir	good evening (meeting and parting)	*ça va?*	how are you? how do you do?	
au revoir	goodbye			
bonne nuit	goodnight	*ça va bien*	I'm fine	
excusez-moi	excuse me, sorry	*comment vous appelez-vous?*	what's your name?	
pardon	excuse me, sorry			
s'il vous plaît	please	*je m'appelle . . .*	my name is . . .	
merci	thank you			

Listening

A ▶ Are these people saying 'Hello' or 'Goodbye'? What time of day is it? Copy the grid into your book. Then listen to the cassette and put a tick in the columns to show. ◀

	Hello	Goodbye	Day	Evening	Night	Didn't say
1						
2						
3						
4						
5						

B ▶ Listen to those five people again: who are they speaking to? Write in your book:

Sir
Madam
Miss

Write numbers 1 – 5 next to the correct word as you listen. ◀

C Here are the English translations of what the next people are saying, but they are in the wrong order. ▶ Write down the letters in the correct order as you hear them. ◀

- a My name is Meunier.
- b How are you?
- c Excuse me!
- d What's your name?
- e I'm fine, thank you.
- f Sorry!

Speaking

A Look at the pictures. Practise the French words. See if you can say them with the speech bubbles covered up.

B Practise them with a partner.

- Read the phrases to each other.
- For the last two pictures, say one of the phrases and see if your partner can give a reply.
- Cover the words, see if your partner can say the right thing. Then get your partner to test you.

C Build up a whole conversation with a partner, using several pictures: a greeting, some questions and answers, goodbye. Remember to use *monsieur*, *madame* or *mademoiselle*. Practise until you can have a short conversation without looking at the pictures.

D A relay race! Try this at the end of a lesson, in groups of five or six.

- The first two in each team say *Bonjour* to each other and shake hands; then the second turns round to the third and they greet each other; then the third turns to the fourth, and so on.
- Next time round, ask *Ça va?* and answer *Ça va bien, merci*.
- The third time, say your name: *Je m'appelle* . . .
- Practise first, then start the race and see which group finishes first!

Reading

Read what these people are saying and answer the questions below.

Give the correct letter to answer these questions:

1. Who is saying goodbye?
2. Who is saying thank you?
3. Who is feeling fine?
4. Who is saying 'excuse me' to a girl?
5. Who is on the phone?
6. Who is greeting a woman?
7. Who is greeting a man?
8. Who is saying good night?
9. Who wants to know someone's name?
10. Who is saying sorry?

Writing

Write down what you will say when . . .

1. you meet someone at:
   9 o'clock in the morning
   2 in the afternoon
   7 o'clock in the evening.

2. you answer the telephone.

3. you want to know someone's name.

4. you are saying goodbye at:
   9 o'clock at night
   midday.

5. you need to apologise.

6. someone has just saved your life.

▶ To sum up . . .

You will find it easier now to make friends and get on well in shops and as you travel.

The French often shake hands when saying *Bonjour* or *Bonsoir*, and polite greetings are used a great deal in everyday life. It is also usual for friends to kiss each other on the cheek when they meet or part.

Now fill in your record sheet.

2 Numbers and prices: 1–69

Learning some numbers is essential if you want to go shopping in France. Once you've learned the numbers up to 20, you'll find it's easy to build all the rest up to 100. This unit will take you up to 69; unit 24 deals with numbers from 70 to 100.

1 un	11 onze	21 vingt et un	30 trente
2 deux	12 douze	22 vingt-deux	40 quarante
3 trois	13 treize	23 vingt-trois	50 cinquante
4 quatre	14 quatorze		60 soixante
5 cinq	15 quinze		
6 six	16 seize		
7 sept	17 dix-sept		
8 huit	18 dix-huit		
9 neuf	19 dix-neuf		
10 dix	20 vingt		

Before listening to the tape, spend some time going over these on your own and with a partner. Look at how 21, 22 and 23 are made up; then work out other numbers up to 69. For example, 24 is *vingt-quatre*, 35 is *trente-cinq*.

Numbers 1–20

Listening

A ▶ You will hear numbers between 1 and 10, in any order. Just write them down in your book in figures as you hear them. ◀

▶ Now you will hear them in sentences. Listen for the number only. Again, write the figures down as you hear them. ◀

B ▶ Now you will hear numbers between 11 and 20. Have another look at them first. Then listen, and do the same as before. ◀

▶ Now numbers 11–20 in sentences. ◀

Speaking

A In a group of four or more, try counting round the group up to 20.

B Work with a partner.
- Take it in turns to say a number; your partner has to write it down. Who can get the most right?
- Or take turns to throw two dice, and say in French what number you get.

Reading and writing

A Write these numbers in figures:

treize	vingt	quatorze
huit	quatre	dix-neuf
un	dix	quinze
	trois	

B Write these numbers in French words:

17   2   16   5   7

11   18   9   12   6

C Write out these sums in figures, and put in the answers:

quatre + dix =
onze + cinq =
vingt − trois =
dix-huit − six =

Numbers 21–69

Now for numbers 21 – 69. You already know 1 – 9: you can add them to the words *vingt* (20), *trente* (30), *quarante* (40), *cinquante* (50) and *soixante* (60) to make numbers up to 69.

Notice that *un* has *et* before it when it goes with another number, so that 31 is *trente et un*.

Listening

A ▶ You will hear numbers between 21 and 40. Just write them in figures as you hear them. ◀

B In France, telephone numbers have eight figures, always given in pairs. 20.35.40.15 would be *vingt trente-cinq quarante quinze*.

▶ Listen to the phone numbers given on the tape and write them down. ◀
The first is done for you:

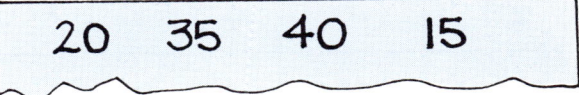

C ▶ Now you will hear numbers between 41 and 69. Write them as you hear them, in figures. ◀

D ▶ These telephone numbers are made up of numbers 40 – 69. Listen and write them down in four pairs, as before. ◀
The first is done for you:

E ▶ Now you are out shopping: you will hear ten prices. For each one, you will hear the number of francs, then the word *francs*, then the number of centimes. Each time, write down the price in figures: so for the first one you will hear *un franc cinquante* and you will write 1,50 F. ◀

F Loto. Play in a large group or a small one of four to six people.

- Divide a piece of paper into twelve squares.

- Write a number in each square. If you're playing in a small group, use numbers between 1 and 30, or between 30 and 69. If you're playing in a large group, use numbers between 1 and 69.

- One person reads out numbers at random, in French. If you hear a number on your card, cross it out.

- The first person to cross out all their numbers calls out *LOTO* and has won the game.

21	3	24	10
4	15	9	1
29	12	27	19

Speaking

A Practise counting from 20 to 69 on your own.

Then count in a group: sit in a circle, each person around the circle has to say the next number.

B Work with a partner.

- Point to one of the price tags on this page. Your partner has to say the price on it. Then swap over. Remember: 1,50 F = *un franc cinquante*.

- Make up a price of your own and say it; see if your partner can write down the figures.

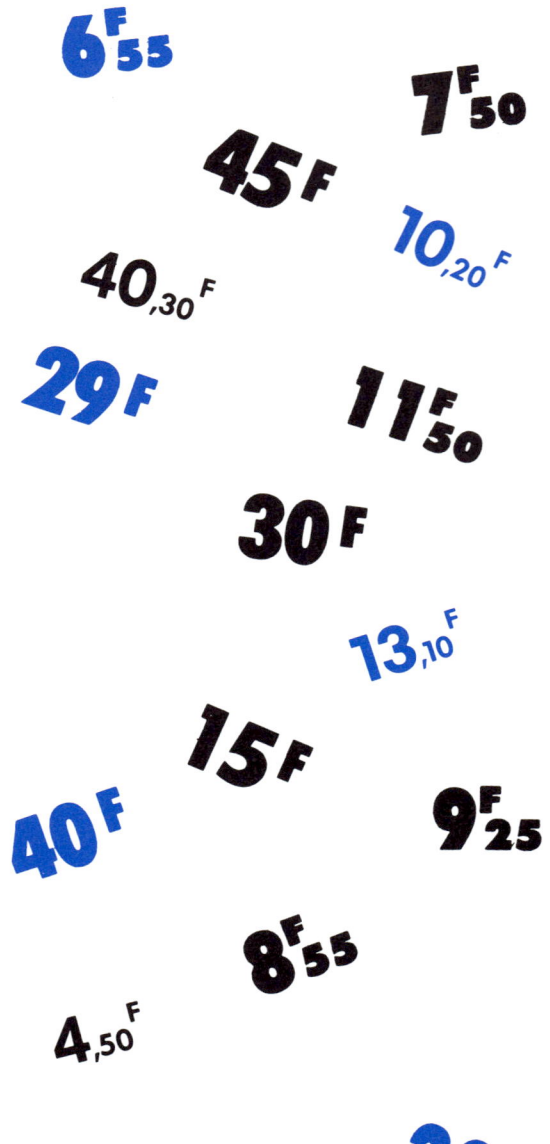

Reading

Write down these prices in figures:

1. vingt francs cinquante
2. treize francs quarante
3. dix-sept francs soixante
4. quinze francs quarante-cinq
5. quatorze francs trente-cinq
6. onze francs cinquante-cinq
7. douze francs trente-cinq
8. seize francs soixante-cinq
9. dix-neuf francs cinquante
10. dix-huit francs dix.

Writing

On a cheque the amount is written out in figures and in words. Can you write out the words in your book to complete these cheques? The first has been done for you.

▶ And finally . . .

Don't worry too much if you don't catch a price in a shop. Just listen for the francs; if there are any centimes, just add an extra franc, and expect a tiny amount of change!

At the time of writing, one franc is worth about 10p, ten centimes are worth only one penny! Of course, you will also need to know the numbers to cope with times, addresses, dates and so on.

Now fill in your record sheet.

⋛3⋛ At the post office

You can sometimes buy stamps from tobacconists, newspaper shops and hotels, but the post office will always have exactly the ones you want.
If you're writing to friends in the UK, it's slightly cheaper to send postcards than letters.

You can also have mail sent to the post office for you to collect, if you aren't staying at a fixed address; you will have to show proof of your identity when you go to collect something.

▶ Words you will need:

la poste	post office	c'est combien?	how much does it cost?
un timbre	stamp		
un timbre-poste	postage stamp	un franc	one franc
		dix centimes	ten centimes
je voudrais	I would like		
envoyer	to send	un, deux,	1 2
une lettre	a letter	trois, quatre,	3 4
une carte postale	a postcard	cinq, six,	5 6
en Grande-Bretagne	to Great Britain	sept, huit,	7 8
en France	to France	neuf, dix	9 10
la boîte aux lettres	the post box	poste restante	the post office department where letters can be kept for you to collect in person

Listening

A ▶ Listen to these seven people at the post office. What are they sending, and where to? Copy the grid into your book going down seven lines. Fill in as much as you can: write the numbers and **F** for France or **GB** for Great Britain. ◀

	Number of letters	Number of postcards	Country
1			

B ▶ These people are all asking something. Look at the pictures. Listen to the cassette and write down the letters in the order you hear them. ◀

C ▶ Write numbers **1 – 6**, and this time as you listen write down *how many stamps* are being bought. ◀

D ▶ Need some practice on prices? Listen to that tape again and try to hear *what values of stamps* they are buying, in francs and centimes. ◀

Reading

A Look at these signs:

Choose the best sign for these people to look for. Write the name and the number of the sign.

Jean	wants to post a letter
Louise	wants to buy some stamps
Angèle	wants to buy postcards
Paul	is picking up some mail
Martine	is looking for a post office
Alex	wants to ask the price of a stamp

B Pick out the words you know to help you complete the sentences. Sylvie Duclos is talking about what she did yesterday.

1. Sylvie went to the ....
2. She wanted to buy ....
3. She was sending a letter to ....
4. She was sending a .... to France.
5. She had to pay: 3,40 F/2,20 F/4,20 F.
6. Lastly, she looked for ....

> D'abord, je suis allée à la poste. Je voulais acheter des timbres pour envoyer une lettre en Grande-Bretagne. J'avais aussi une carte postale pour la France. J'ai payé quatre francs vingt. Ensuite, j'ai cherché la boîte aux lettres.

Speaking

A

1 – Voilà la poste!

2 – Je voudrais des timbres, s'il vous plaît.

3 – Une lettre pour la Grande-Bretagne?
– Oui. Et une carte postale.

4 – C'est combien?
– C'est quatre francs vingt.

5 – Une lettre pour Martin Jones, s'il vous plaît?
– Pour Martin Jones? Non!

6 – Où est la boîte aux lettres, s'il vous plaît?

How many of these can you say in French?

1 – There's the post office!
2 – I'd like some stamps, please.
3 – A letter for Great Britain?
– Yes. And a postcard.
4 – How much is that?
– That's 4 francs 20.
5 – A letter for Martin Jones, please?
– For Martin Jones? No.
6 – Where is the postbox, please?

B Work out and say as many different sentences as you can, using this table. Use one set of words from each box.

Je voudrais envoyer	une lettre deux lettres trois lettres une carte postale deux cartes postales trois cartes postales	en France en Grande-Bretagne	s'il vous plaît

C Ask in French how to find the things shown in these photos. Use *Où est . . .?* and don't forget *s'il vous plaît*.

Writing

A Find and write down the post office words:

TIMBREPOSTELETTREBOÎTEAUXLETTRESENVOYERPOSTERESTANTECARTEPOSTALEPOSTE

B Your mate at work can't speak French. Write down a message for her to give to the post office clerk. Just use what you have learned in this unit.

She'd like
– two stamps for letters to Great Britain
– three stamps for postcards to Great Britain
– one stamp for a letter to France and . . .
– she'd like to know if there are any letters for her.

> ▶ **And to sum up . . .**
>
> Now you can find a post office and buy stamps.
>
> Fill in your record sheet.

⊰4⊱ At the restaurant

Best value and simplest to order is the *Prix Fixe* menu, where you pay a fixed price for three or four courses: a small starter, a main dish, sometimes cheese, then a dessert or fruit. Sometimes drinks are included, perhaps a quarter litre of wine. Fresh bread and water are on the table, and you should not need to ask for them.

When you arrive, ask the waiter or waitress for a table for the number in your party: *Pour quatre, s'il vous plaît. Pour deux, s'il vous plaît.*

▶ **Words you will need:**

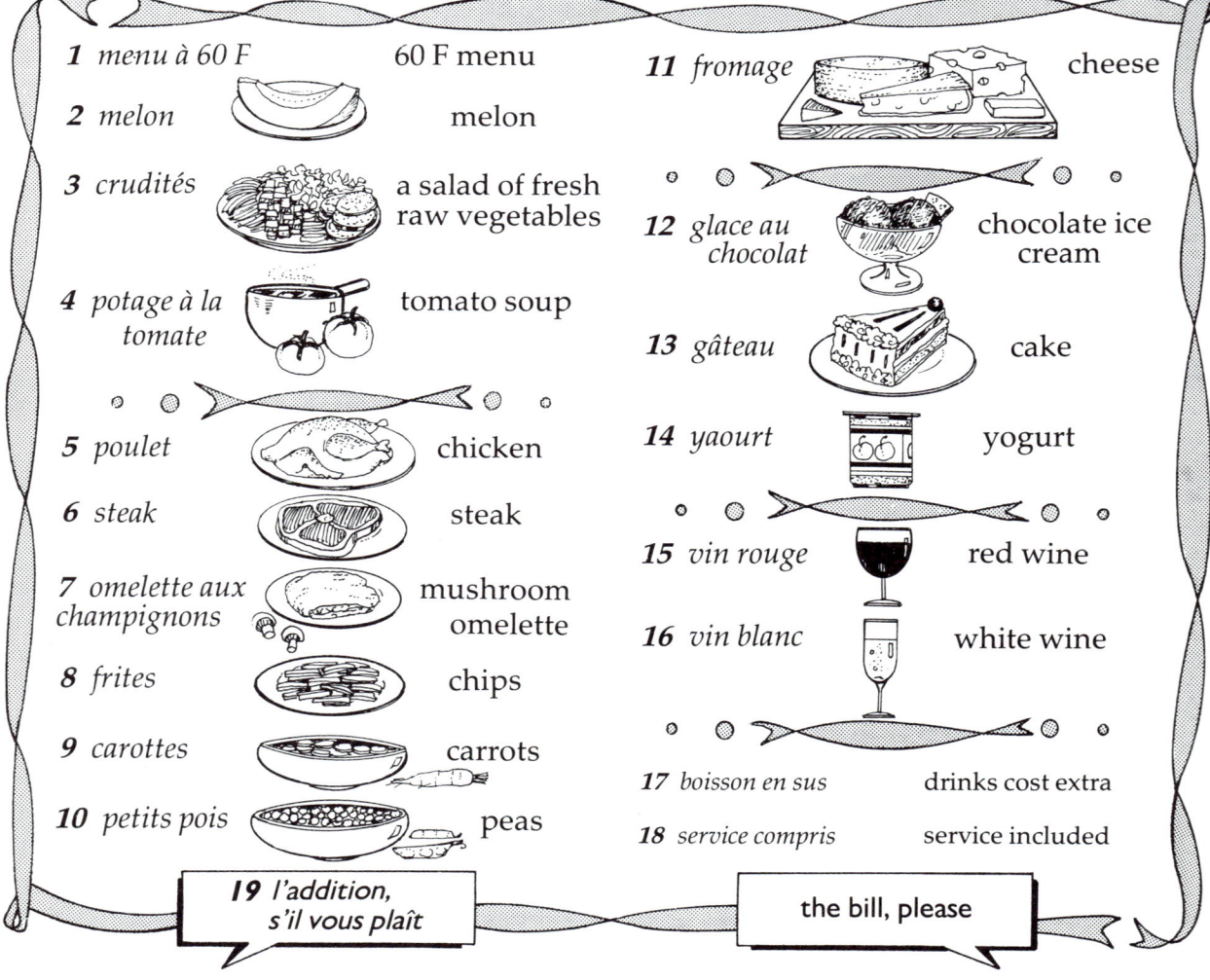

1 *menu à 60 F* — 60 F menu
2 *melon* — melon
3 *crudités* — a salad of fresh raw vegetables
4 *potage à la tomate* — tomato soup
5 *poulet* — chicken
6 *steak* — steak
7 *omelette aux champignons* — mushroom omelette
8 *frites* — chips
9 *carottes* — carrots
10 *petits pois* — peas
11 *fromage* — cheese
12 *glace au chocolat* — chocolate ice cream
13 *gâteau* — cake
14 *yaourt* — yogurt
15 *vin rouge* — red wine
16 *vin blanc* — white wine
17 *boisson en sus* — drinks cost extra
18 *service compris* — service included
19 *l'addition, s'il vous plaît* — the bill, please

Listening

A ▶ Listen to these people ordering a starter, a main dish or a vegetable, or asking for the 60 franc menu.

Put **1 – 10** in your book, and then for each item write the correct number from the menu on the opposite page. ◀

B ▶ Now listen to people ordering desserts or drinks, or asking for the bill. Put **1 – 8** in your book, and as you listen, put the correct number from the menu opposite. ◀

C ▶ Now you will hear three people ordering a meal. Each will choose six things. Listen for the food items, and write down the numbers from the menu for each person. ◀

D ▶ The person you will hear next has finished his meal and is asking for the bill. Listen to the tape and answer these questions with *yes* or *no*. ◀

1 Is service included in the cost?
2 Do drinks cost extra here?

Speaking

A Use the menu and practise saying the name of each item.

- Practise asking for the fixed-price meal – *Le menu à soixante francs, s'il vous plaît* and asking for the bill – *L'addition, s'il vous plaît*.

- See if you can just look at the pictures and still say the right word.

B Now work with a partner. Use the menu to order a meal.

- Begin by asking for *Le menu à soixante francs, s'il vous plaît*.

- Choose a meal for yourself: a starter, a main course, a vegetable, a sweet, and a drink.

- Let your partner point to the pictures as you say the words, to show that they can understand you.

- Finish by asking for the bill: *L'addition, s'il vous plaît*.

- Then it's your partner's turn to order a meal, and your turn to point to the pictures.

C Give your partner five numbers from the menu, one from each course. They have to order that meal. Then they can do the same for you.

Reading

A Copy out these sentences, choosing the correct way to end them from the two you are given.

1 *Menu Prix Fixe* means that
 a) you pay one price for all the courses.
 b) each item has its own price.

2 *Boisson en sus* means that
 a) your drink is included in the price.
 b) you pay extra for a drink.

3 *Service compris* means that
 a) service is included.
 b) you pay an extra service charge.

4 *Boisson comprise* means that
 a) your drink is included in the price.
 b) you pay extra for drinks.

B Look at these bills.

L'ESCARGOT
Table no. 4
Menu à 60F
melon
poulet
carottes
yaourt
vin blanc 10F
Total: 70F

L'ESCARGOT
Table no. 7
Menu à 60F
crudités
omelette aux champignons
petits pois
fromage
glace au chocolat
vin blanc (10F)
Total: 70F

L'ESCARGOT
Table no. 9
Menu à 60F
potage à la tomate
steak
frites
fromage
gâteau
vin rouge (10F)
Total: 70F

Answer these questions by giving the table number shown on the bill.

a Who had red wine?
b Who had soup?
c Who did not have cheese?
d Who had chicken?
e Who had vegetable salad?
f Who had chips?
g Who had peas?
h Which bill is for someone on a diet?
i Which is for a vegetarian?
j Which is for someone who likes a big, filling dinner?

Writing

A Make up two meals of your own from the 60 franc menu on page 14. One meal you would most like to have, and one you would most dislike. Write them out in French in your book.

> **▶ Summary**
>
> You can now order a meal. There may be many things on a menu you won't know, but you should understand enough to get something to eat!
>
> A hint: in Paris, tourist hot-spot restaurants are expensive. You'll find cheaper ones tucked away: an up-to-date guide book will give you some ideas of where to look.
>
> Now fill in your record sheet.

B Write in French the words that mean:

1. Drinks cost extra.
2. The bill, please.
3. Service included.
4. Fixed-price menu.

▶5▶ At the campsite

If you book a package holiday at a French campsite, your travel agent can make the bookings for you. Or you might prefer to tour part of France and find space on campsites as you go.

French campsites are graded in the same way as hotels, one-star to four-stars. You can probably find a guide in your local bookshop or library, or you could write to the French Government Tourist Office (178 Piccadilly, London W1V 0AL) for a list.

▶ **Words you will need:**

un camping	a campsite	où est . . . ?	where is . . . ?
vous avez de la place?	do you have any space?	la réception	reception
		l'emplacement	the space for a tent
pour combien de nuits?	for how many nights?	le bloc sanitaire	the building with toilets, showers and washrooms
pour une nuit	for one night		
pour deux nuits	for two nights	la salle de jeux	the games room
pour une tente	for a tent	où sont . . . ?	where are . . . ?
pour une caravane	for a caravan	les douches	the showers
pour combien de personnes?	for how many people?	les toilettes	the toilets
pour trois personnes	for three people	les machines à laver	the washing machines

Listening

A ▶ Write numbers **1–4** in your book. Listen to these people booking in at a campsite. Write down how many nights they want to stay. ◀

▶ Now listen again, to find out if they are booking for a tent or caravan. Write **T** for tent and **C** for caravan. ◀

B ▶ Write **1–6** in your book. Listen to the receptionist asking questions. Look at these English questions and write down the letter of the one you hear, beside each number. (You will hear some of the questions more than once.) ◀

   a How many nights do you want?
   b For how many people?
   c Is it for a tent?
   d Is it for a caravan?

C Look at the pictures.
▶ Then listen to the tape: seven people are looking for something on a campsite. Listen to their questions and write the letters from the pictures to match what you hear. ◀

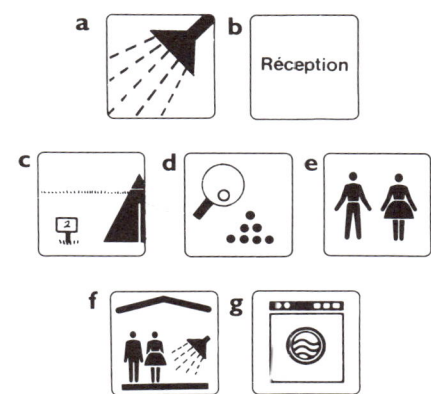

Speaking

A Look at the French phrases here and on the next page. Practise saying them until you can do them just by looking at the English captions underneath.

Then work with a partner. Point to one of the English speech bubbles and see if they can say the right thing in French. See how many you can get right!

C'est pour une caravane! — It's for a caravan!
C'est pour une tente! — It's for a tent!
Non, pour deux nuits! — No, for two nights!
Vous avez de la place? — Have you any room?
Oui, pour une nuit! — Yes, for one night!
Non, pour trois personnes! — No, for three people!

Now they've booked in and they want to know where everything is . . . Do the same as you did with the picture on page 19.

B Try booking in at reception. The grid opposite tells you what to ask for. So, for example, for the first one you could start off with *Vous avez de la place?* and then you would say:

C'est pour une nuit . . . pour une tente . . . pour une personne.

☾	▲🚐	👥
1	T	1
1	T	2
1	C	2
3	C	3
2	T	1
7	T	4

C Look at the seven pictures in Listening task C on page 19. You are on a campsite looking for those places: can you ask seven questions to help you find them?

Reading

A Can you find nine campsite terms here? Write them down in English, in any order.

B Find the word you will look for when . . .

1 you're looking for the toilets.
2 you want to find your tent space.
3 you want a shower.
4 you need to sign in.
5 you want a game of table tennis.
6 you need to wash your clothes.
7 you want the toilets, showers and washing facilities.

a Réception
b Emplacement
c Machines à laver
d Toilettes
e Bloc sanitaire
f Salle de jeux
g Douches

C

Camping de Joinville
* *

21 emplacements pour tentes
toilettes, douches
salle de jeux

BIENVENUE!

Look at this sign and then copy out and complete the following sentences.

The name of the campsite is . . . .
There are . . . . . . tent spaces.
They have toilets and . . . . . . and . . . . . .

Writing

A Can you fill in the missing letters on these campsite words?

1 _AR_ _AN_
2 _E_ _E
3 E_ _A_E_ _
4 _ _IL_ _T_S
5 _ _ _ _ SAN_ _AIR_
6 MA_ _ _ _ES L_ _ _R
7 R_C_P_ _N
8 D_ _CH_

B This advert is not complete. Copy it out, changing the symbols to French words to finish it off.

C You get a job working on a campsite in the South of England, where there are lots of French tourists. The owner asks you to write out a short advert for it, in French.

Use the advert you have just corrected in B. **Change** what you need to, and **leave out** what you do not need.

☐ It is called 'Stone Farm Campsite'.
☐ The address is Stone Lane, Dover.
☐ It has space for 12 tents but does not take caravans.
☐ It has showers, toilets and one washing machine.
☐ It has no games room.

> ▶ **And to sum up . . .**
>
> You should now feel at home on a French campsite.
>
> Look back at what you have done, then fill in your record sheet.

6 Train travel

Travelling by train is an excellent way of getting around in France. Buying tickets and finding the right train is not difficult if you know a few phrases.

The TGV goes at up to 300 km per hour on certain routes: it's very modern and comfortable but you'll have to reserve a seat and at busy times you'll have to pay a £4–£6 supplement. Treat yourself!

▶ **Words you will need:**

la gare	the station	un aller simple	a single
quel quai?	which platform?	un aller-retour	a return
quai numéro un	platform number 1	pour Paris	to Paris
		deuxième classe	second class
un, deux,	1 2		
trois, quatre,	3 4	les bagages	luggage
cinq, six,	5 6	billets	tickets
sept, huit,	7 8	fumeur	smoking
neuf, dix	9 10	non-fumeur	non-smoking
		un horaire	timetable
		TGV	high-speed train

Listening

A ▶ On the tape you will hear the words shown under the pictures, either on their own or in sentences. First write **1 – 12** in your book; then as you hear each one, write the correct letter **a – f** ◀

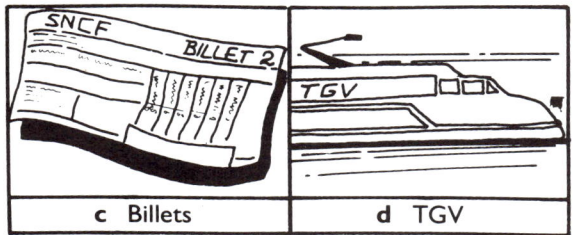

a Bagages
b Gare
c Billets
d TGV
e Horaire
f Quai

B ▶ Which platform will your train go from? Listen to these questions and answers, and write down the platform number given in the answer. ◀

C ▶ These people are all going to Paris, but what kind of tickets are they buying?

- Copy this grid into your book.
- Then listen to the tape.
- Put a tick in the grid when you hear what kind of ticket or what compartment the speaker wants. You may need more than one tick for each ticket. ◀

	Single	Return	2nd Class	Smoking	Non-Smoking
1					
2					
3					
4					
5					
6					
7					
8					
9					
10					

Speaking

A Practise asking for your platform: *Quel quai?* Work with a partner. Take it in turn, one of you asking *Quel quai?* and the other replying *Quai numéro . . .*

- You could throw a die to decide the number, like this:

  Partner 1: *Quel quai, s'il vous plaît?*
  Partner 2 throws die: *Quai numéro deux.*

- Or the one who asks *Quel quai?* writes down the number when they hear it, to show that they understand. Like this:

  Partner 1: *Quel quai, s'il vous plaît?*
  Partner 2: *Quai numéro six.*
  So partner 1 writes down 6.

B Look at these symbols.

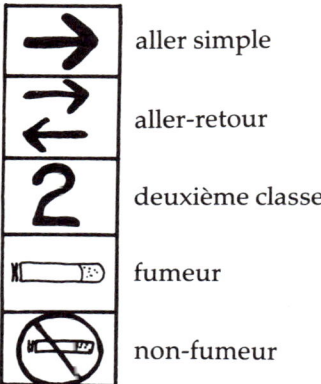

- → aller simple
- ⇄ aller-retour
- 2 deuxième classe
- 🚬 fumeur
- 🚭 non-fumeur

Can you ask for these tickets?

1 Un → pour Paris, s'il vous plaît.
2 Un ⇄ pour Paris, s'il vous plaît.
3 Un aller simple pour Paris, s'il vous plaît, 🚬
4 Un aller-retour pour Paris, s'il vous plaît, 🚭
5 Un aller-retour pour Paris, s'il vous plaît, 2

Take it in turns to say these sentences, in any order, to a partner. Do they understand what you want?

C Work with a partner. Point to one or two of the symbols in B, and see if your partner can ask for that ticket. Then swap over. Which of you can get the most right?

> **HINT:**
> When you ask for a ticket in France, they will tell you the price. Don't worry if you don't understand at first: just read the number of francs from the till, or ask them to repeat: *Comment?* or *Pardon?*

D You may want to go somewhere else!

Instead of saying *Un aller simple pour PARIS, s'il vous plaît*, ask for a ticket for these places, using the same sentence, but taking PARIS out and putting the new place in.

1 Marseille
2 Tours
3 Toulouse
4 Orléans

E

les bagages | le TGV
un horaire | le quai
un aller simple | un aller-retour

Look at these pictures. Say what they show, in French. Can you do it with the labels covered up? Try testing each other.

Reading

A Here are some signs you might see in a station.

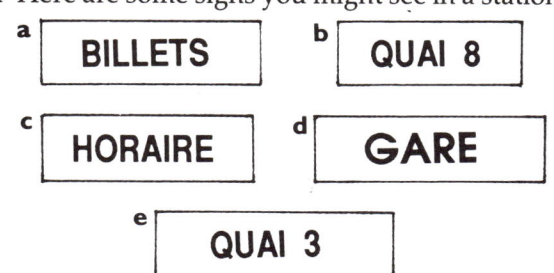

Answer these questions by writing down the right letter.

1 You need platform 8. Which sign?
2 You want the station. Which sign?
3 You want a ticket. Which sign?
4 You want platform 3. Which sign?
5 You need a timetable. Which sign?

B Remember the symbols on page 24? Read these sentences. What kind of ticket is being asked for? Put **1 – 5** in your book and draw the correct symbol (or symbols) next to each number.

1 Un aller-retour pour Paris, s'il vous plaît.
2 Un aller simple en deuxième classe pour Dieppe, s'il vous plaît.
3 Un aller-retour pour Toulouse, s'il vous plaît, non-fumeur.
4 Un aller simple pour Bordeaux, s'il vous plaît.
5 Un aller-retour pour Calais, s'il vous plaît, fumeur.

C Can you find eight words from this unit? List them in your book. Work in pairs or threes if you like.

Q	U	S	T	E	L	L	I	B	E	L
B	I	L	L	R	S	Q	R	T	O	T
A	R	O	T	I	Z	U	U	H	O	G
G	R	E	U	A	N	A	E	I	L	V
A	L	L	E	R	S	I	M	P	L	E
G	H	E	T	O	U	I	U	R	S	G
E	N	O	N	H	E	N	F	I	A	X
S	O	I	T	J	V	G	A	R	E	N

Writing

A These sentences have some symbols instead of words. Copy them, changing the symbols into the correct French words.

1 Un ➔ pour Paris, s'il vous plaît.
2 Un ⇄ pour Lyon, s'il vous plaît.
3 Un aller simple en 2 pour Nice, s'il vous plaît.
4 Un ⇄ pour Londres, s'il vous plaît.
5 Un aller simple pour Calais, s'il vous plaît, 🚬
6 Un ➔ pour Orléans, s'il vous plaît, 🚭

B These words are mixed up: write them out correctly in French.

Then, next to each one put the matching English word from the ones below.

PLATFORM   TICKETS   LUGGAGE

TIMETABLE   STATION

> ▶ **And finally . . .**
>
> You should have no difficulty now in travelling by train in France.
>
> Fill in your record sheet now.

7 At the bank

Before you go abroad you will probably change some cash into foreign currency. But most of your money should be in traveller's cheques to make it easier and safer to carry around. You probably need to go to a French bank to change them, or to change English money into francs. Take your passport with you!

The bank will make a small charge for changing your money.

▶ **Words you will need:**

la banque	bank	des livres sterling	pounds sterling (£)
le crédit	you might see this word in the name of a bank	un chèque de voyage	a traveller's cheque
le bureau de change	you can change money here	remplir cette fiche	to fill in this form
change		le passeport	passport
je voudrais	I'd like	le nom	name
changer de l'argent	to change some money	l'adresse en France	address in France
en francs	into francs	des billets	notes
		des pièces	coins
		de la monnaie	change

Reading

A Which of these signs will you look for when you want to change some money?

B

a

b

c

There are 100 centimes in a franc. For **a**, **b** and **c**, how much do the notes and coins come to in total?

C Find out how much a franc is worth now in pence. Then try and work out how much the money in B is worth in £ and p.

Listening

A ▶ Listen to these people changing money or traveller's cheques. Can you hear them say *Je voudrais changer . . .?*

Then copy this grid, listen again and put a tick in the columns, to show exactly what they want to do. ◀

	Change cash?	Change traveller's cheques?	Into francs?	Into pounds?
1				
2				
3				

B You will have to fill in a form. The bank clerk will probably do this for you. You need your passport.

▶ Listen to these three conversations; can you understand the bank clerk's questions and instructions?
Write
  F when you hear the bank clerk say they have to fill in the form,
  P when you hear him ask for the passport,
  N for the name and
  A for the address. ◀

C Lastly, they may ask you how you want the money, and you may need some change.
▶ Write numbers **1 – 6**, then fill in
  N when you hear someone ask for notes,
  C when they ask for coins,
  CH when they ask for change. ◀

Speaking

A When you need to change money, what will you say at the bank counter? Make three possible sentences from this table.

Je voudrais changer	de l'argent / des livres sterling / un chèque de voyage	en francs.

Now look at the three pictures.

- You need to change each of these into francs: what do you say?
- Can you do this without using the table to help you, looking only at the pictures?

B

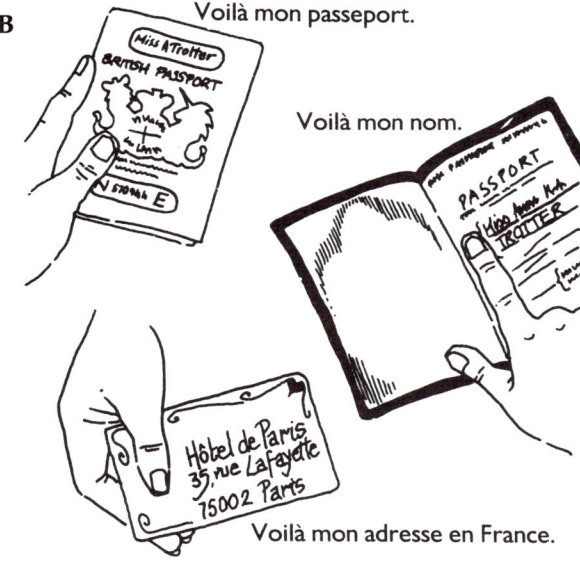

Voilà mon passeport.
Voilà mon nom.
Voilà mon adresse en France.

- Can you say these?
- Cover up the words and say them again.
- Work with a partner: cover up the words and see if they can say the right words for each picture.

C Can you ask for change?

- Practise the French phrases.
- Then work with your partner. Point to an English phrase; can they say it in French? Then swap over.

De la monnaie, s'il vous plaît.
Some change, please.

Des billets, s'il vous plaît.
Some notes, please.

Des pièces, s'il vous plaît.
Some coins, please.

Writing

A Can you unjumble these?

QHÈEUC ED GAVOYE   TIRÉDC
    UBAREU ED GENAHC   QUEBNA
TIBSLEL
    SCEPIÈ
STOPSPARE   MON
        SCARNF
    GERANT

B Copy out these sentences and fill in the gaps:

1 Je voudrais _ _ _ _ _ _ _ de l'argent.
2 Un chèque de _ _ _ _ _ _.
3 De la m _ _ _ _ _ _ s'il vous plaît.
4 Voilà mon p_ _ _ _ _ _ _ _.
5 Voilà _ _ _ _ _ _ _ _ _ _ en France.

C You are on holiday with your friend in Paris and she has to go to the bank. Write down what she will have to say. She wants to

- change some money
- and a traveller's cheque
- into francs.
- She also wants some change – in coins.

> ▶ **And to sum up . . .**
>
> You should be able to change your money now. Try and work out the exchange rate if you can, it will help you take care of your money better.
>
> Now fill in your record sheet.

8 The weather

▶ **Words you will need:**

le temps	the weather
quel temps fait-il?	what's the weather like?
il fait beau	it's good
il fait mauvais	it's bad
il fait chaud	it's hot
il fait froid	it's cold
il fait du soleil	it's sunny
il fait du vent	it's windy
il fait du brouillard	it's foggy
il neige	it's snowing
il pleut	it's raining
il gèle	it's freezing
la météo	the weather forecast

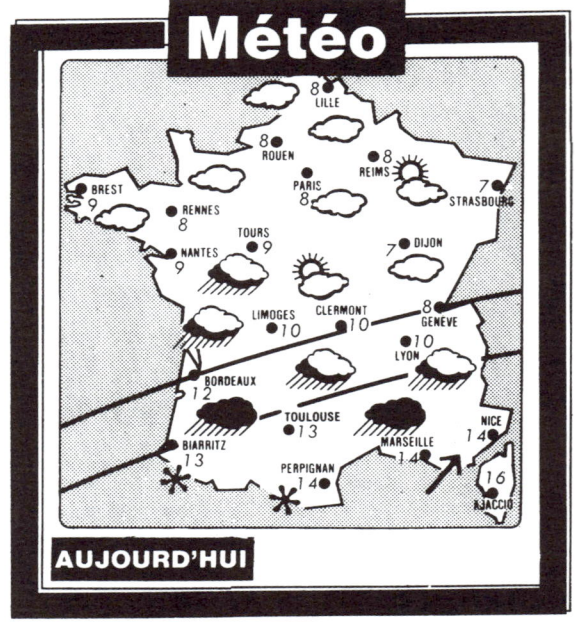

Listening

A First list in your book the words on the right.

▶ Now listen to the tape: there are ten items. Write the numbers next to the right words in your book. Number 1 has been done, to help you. ◀

```
hot
good
weather  1
bad
cold
```

B Look at these weather signs:

▶ List **1 – 12** in your book. Listen to the tape and quickly sketch the right sign next to each number. ◀

C Now the weather forecast: you might need to listen to this, on French radio, especially if you're travelling. Because the forecast is talking about the next day or some time in the future, some of the words – the verbs – may have different endings. Don't worry! Just listen for the sounds you have already learned.

First list these words in your book:

```
forecast    bad
wind        hot
rain        cold
sun         snow
fog         freezing
good
```

▶ Listen to the tape, and write the correct number next to the words. ◀

D ▶ List **1 – 6** in your book. Read these questions and answer **yes** or **no** next to the number in your book, as you listen to the tape. ◀

1 Is it safe to travel in Normandy tomorrow?
2 Will you be able to ski in the Alps?
3 Will it be good sunbathing weather at Bordeaux?
4 Will you need warm clothes in the Pyrenees?
5 Will you need an umbrella in Paris?
6 A day for wellies in Nice?

Speaking

A Look at the pictures below. Beneath them you will see a question and several answers. Three of the answers are true, the other is false.

Quel temps fait-il?   Il fait chaud.
　　　　　　　　　　　Il fait froid.
　　　　　　　　　　　Il neige.
　　　　　　　　　　　Il gèle.

Quel temps fait-il?   Il fait chaud.
　　　　　　　　　　　Il fait du soleil.
　　　　　　　　　　　Il pleut.
　　　　　　　　　　　Il fait beau.

Quel temps fait-il?   Il fait mauvais.
　　　　　　　　　　　Il fait du vent.
　　　　　　　　　　　Il fait du soleil.
　　　　　　　　　　　Il pleut.

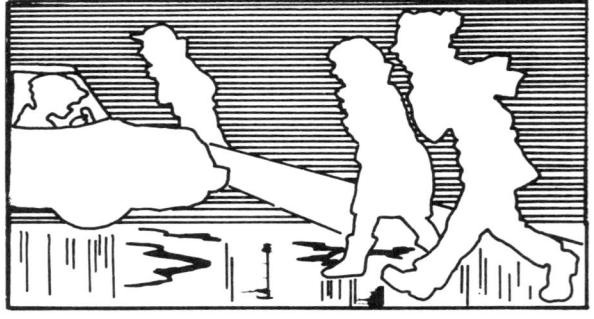

Quel temps fait-il?   Il fait beau.
　　　　　　　　　　　Il fait du brouillard.
　　　　　　　　　　　Il gèle.
　　　　　　　　　　　Il fait mauvais.

- Learn the question and one true answer for each picture. Practise saying them with the writing covered up.
- See how many other true answers you can learn for each picture; practise saying them.
- Then find a partner, and take it in turns to ask and answer for each picture. How many can you do? Can you do them with the writing covered up?

B Play a guessing game with a partner.
- Draw a weather symbol like the ones in Listening task B, or write a word, such as hot, cold, good, bad.
- Cover it up and ask *Quel temps fait-il?*
- See if your partner can guess what you have chosen, guessing in French using the sentences you learned in A.
- Then swap over.

Reading

A It might be helpful to be able to read weather forecasts in French newspapers. Again, just look for the words you have learned, such as *du soleil* and *froid*. Don't be put off if *il fait* has become *il fera* and *il neige* has become *il neigera* (this is the future tense, used to talk about something that will happen).

Here are the weather forecasts for some places in France.

> **Paris.** Il fera du soleil, mais il fera froid.
> **St Malo.** Il fera beau: il fera du soleil.
> **La Baule.** Il pleuvra, et il fera du vent.
> **Toulouse.** Il fera froid, avec beaucoup de vent.
> **St Tropez.** Il fera beau et chaud.
> **Lyon.** Il fera mauvais: il fera du brouillard.
> **Les Alpes.** Il neigera, et il fera très froid.
> **Rouen.** Il fera du brouillard, et il pleuvra.
> **Strasbourg.** Il neigera, mais il fera beau plus tard.
> **Boulogne.** Il gèlera, et il fera froid.

- Copy the boxes below into your book. Each one matches one of the places in the list above.
- Write next to each box, the name of the place which will get weather like that tomorrow.

B Write in English ten short sentences, one for each place in task A, saying what weather they can expect. Here is the first one for you:

> In Paris it will be sunny and cold.

Writing

Divide a page of your book into ten sections. In each, write a weather sentence in French, and illustrate it. Either with a simple weather sign or a picture, depending on how good you are at drawing!

▶ To sum up...

You should now be able to talk about the weather, and use French weather forecasts to some extent. You'll find that the British are not the only ones who like to discuss the weather!

Fill in your record sheet now.

9 Asking the way

Asking the way is really not too difficult. Understanding the answer is much harder! Once you can ask for the places in this unit, you'll find you can ask for all sorts of other places, things or people too.

▶ **Words you will need:**

pardon	excuse me
où est . . .?	where is . . .?
voilà!	there it is!
je ne sais pas	I don't know
le supermarché	supermarket
la pâtisserie	cake shop
la boulangerie	bread shop, bakery
l'office de tourisme	tourist information office
la poste	post office
la banque	bank
le camping	campsite
l'hôtel	hotel
l'auberge de jeunesse	youth hostel
le parking	car park
la station-service	petrol station
la gare	train station
où sont les WC?	where are the toilets?

Listening

A ▶ You will hear people asking the way to these places. Copy the names out first, then write the numbers next to them as you listen. ◀

CAMPING

POSTE

HÔTEL PAX

PARKING

GARE

PÂTISSERIE

B ▶ Play the tape again. Listen carefully for *Où est . . .?* ◀

C You may hear other ways of asking the way, but you can always rely on *Où est . . .?* ▶ Listen to these other ways of asking. ◀

▶ Now listen to that tape again. Which places were they asking for? Write the correct word, chosen from each group of three. ◀

1	Hotel	Tourist office	Bank
2	Baker's	Petrol station	Post office
3	Youth hostel	Station	Supermarket
4	Cake shop	Supermarket	Car park
5	Toilets	Campsite	Hotel
6	Bank	Tourist office	Cake shop
7	Hotel	Bread shop	Campsite

D ▶ The people you will hear next don't know much! Copy these words (or the first few letters of them). As you listen to the tape, number them correctly in the order you hear them. ◀

BANQUE

AUBERGE de JEUNESSE

BOULANGERIE

STATION-SERVICE

SUPERMARCHÉ

WC

Speaking

A

1 – Excuse me ...

2 – Where's the cake shop?
  – Oh ... I don't know.

3 – Excuse me, where's the station?
  – The station? There's the station!

4 – Where's the tourist office?
  – I don't know!

5 – Where's the supermarket?
  – There it is!

6 – A campsite? I don't know!

Learn these one by one. See how many you can say without looking at the French.

B Find someone to work with. Be helpful! Every time they ask for something, say 'It's right there!'

Example:
  Où est le camping?
  Le camping? Voilà!

C Now you've just arrived in a new town, so you can't help! Whatever you are asked – you don't know!

Example:
  Pardon, où est la gare?
  La gare? Je ne sais pas!

Reading

A Match up the words in these two lists:

1	boulangerie	a	petrol station
2	camping	b	post office
3	auberge de jeunesse	c	car park
4	office de tourisme	d	bread shop
5	station-service	e	train station
6	WC	f	youth hostel
7	banque	g	cake shop
8	pâtisserie	h	tourist office
9	gare	i	campsite
10	parking	j	toilets
11	poste	k	bank

B

a POSTE

b OFFICE DE TOURISME

c BOULANGERIE

d SUPERMARCHÉ

e HÔTEL

f STATION-SERVICE

Find the sign you need when . . .

1 you need some bread for a picnic.
2 you're running out of petrol.
3 you want to buy some cheese and orange juice.
4 you need to buy a street plan.
5 you want some stamps.
6 you need somewhere to spend the night.

C Can you find 11 words from this unit here?

H	G	N	I	P	M	A	C	Y	H	S
O	B	A	N	C	H	U	X	Ô	E	T
T	N	S	P	A	S	B	T	R	V	A
P	Â	T	I	S	S	E	R	I	E	T
O	P	A	M	P	L	R	C	A	R	B
S	I	T	A	S	I	G	R	I	A	A
T	N	I	S	T	E	E	E	C	G	N
E	G	O	S	E	R	V	I	C	E	Q
G	G	N	I	K	R	A	P	L	E	U
R	A	E	T	O	U	R	I	S	M	E

Writing

A Fill in the missing letters to make words from this unit:

1 LA _ _S_ _

2 L'_ _ _ _C_ DE _O_R_ _ _ _

3 LE _U_ _ _M_ _H_

4 LA _ _A_L_ S_R_ _ _E

5 L'_ _B_ _G_ DE _EU_ _ _ _E

6 LA _ _ _L_ _ _ER_ _

B Write down the French sign you would look for . . .

1 to get tourist information.
2 to buy bread.
3 when you want to change money.
4 to get petrol.
5 for a youth hostel.
6 to park your car.

> ▶ **And finally . . .**
>
> You should now be able to ask the way. Of course, you will have to understand the directions people give you! Unit 25 will help you with this.
>
> Now fill in your record sheet.

▶10◀ Café and snack bar

▶ **Words you will need:**

un croque-monsieur	toasted cheese and ham sandwich	un café	black coffee
		un thé	tea without milk
		un café au lait	white coffee
une omelette	omelette	un thé au lait	tea with milk
des frites	chips	une bière	beer
des chips	crisps	un coca	Coca-Cola
un sandwich . . .	. . . sandwich	une limonade	lemonade
au saucisson	salami	un Orangina	fizzy orange drink
au fromage	cheese		
au jambon	ham	s'il vous plaît	please

When you buy food or drink there may be a TARIF or price list on display or on your table, so you can work out the right money to give in advance. However, 15% may be added to that as a service charge. Don't worry about the prices for the moment: we'll concentrate on the food!

Listening

A Here is a sandwich stand menu.

▶ Put **1–7** in your book and listen to the tape. You will hear the names of things on the menu. For each one, just put down the letter of the item you hear. ◀

B ▶ Now you will hear three people ordering a drink and some food from that menu: two items each. Write **1–3** in your book, and for each one write down the letters for whatever they order. ◀

C Here is a café menu.

▶ Put **1–6** in your book and listen to the cassette. Write down the letter of the items you hear. ◀

D ▶ Now you will hear three people ordering food and drink from that café: two items each. Write **1–3** in your book, and then put the right letters for whatever they order, next to each number. ◀

Speaking

A Practise the words on the sandwich stand menu. Then work with a partner.

- One orders a drink and something to eat, the other points to the pictures on the menu to show they have understood.
- Don't forget to add *monsieur*, *madame*, or *mademoiselle* and *s'il vous plaît*.
- Then it's the other one's turn to order.

B Choose the letters of two items for your partner to order; then swap over.

C Now do the same with the café menu. This time, one orders food and a drink, the other is the waiter or waitress and repeats the order to make sure they've got it right.

Reading

A Look again at the sandwich stand menu. How much . . .

1. are the crisps?
2. is the Coca-Cola?
3. is the ham sandwich?
4. is the orange drink?
5. is the salami sandwich?
6. is the lemonade?

B Now look again at the café menu. Answer these questions.

1. How much is the tea?
2. How much is a toasted cheese and ham sandwich?
3. How much is the beer?
4. How much is the omelette?
5. How much is the coffee?
6. How much are the chips?

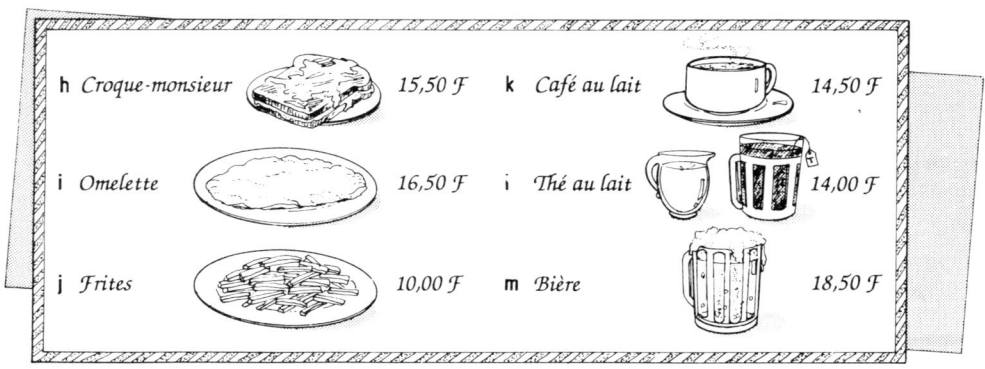

Writing

You will need to look at both menus for this.

Six people want some food and drink, as listed below. Write down in French what they must look for on the menu.

1 Coffee and a cheese sandwich.
2 Crisps and Coca-Cola.
3 Cheese and ham toasted sandwich and a cup of tea.
4 Chips and fizzy orange.
5 Salami sandwich and a beer.
6 An omelette and lemonade.

Time for a drink?

Get together in a group of four to six.

- All except one sit around a table.
- One person is the waiter or waitress and takes the orders from everyone else.
- Each one asks for two items; the waiter has to listen and remember everything that is ordered.
- When you've all chosen, see how much the waiter can remember!
- Then change over: someone else becomes the waiter or waitress.

Or work with a partner.

- Choose one of the menus, order a drink and something to eat.
- Your partner is the waiter or waitress; they repeat your order to check they've got it right.
- Then they ask for payment, *Dix francs, s'il vous plaît*. And you can say thank you, *merci*.
- Then swap roles.

▶ Summary

You should not have to starve between meals!

If you prefer black coffee or tea, just ask for *un café* or *un thé*. Drinks can be dear in cafés; you can buy canned drinks more cheaply from supermarkets, but of course you don't get a seat.

Now fill in your record sheet.

≡ / / ≡ At the tourist information office

When you're on holiday in France, sooner or later you will need a tourist office. Most towns have one, close to the centre and easy to find.

▶ **Words you will need:**

le syndicat d'initiative (SI)	tourist information office	*une liste*	a list
l'office de tourisme	tourist information office	*des restaurants*	of restaurants
		des hôtels	of hotels
		des campings	of campsites
		des monuments	of things to see
		des musées	of museums
un plan de la ville	town plan	*des visites*	of tours
un horaire des autobus	bus timetable	*des distractions*	of things to do
un horaire des trains	train timetable		

Reading

A Look at these signs. Write down the numbers of the ones where you will get tourist information.

1  CREDIT LYONNAIS

2  SYNDICAT d'INITIATIVE

3  OFFICE DE TOURISME

4 **change**

B Once you've found the tourist office, you'll probably find it easiest to look for the information you want yourself.

Look at these leaflets and match them up with the information you need (see list opposite). Write only the letter and the number.

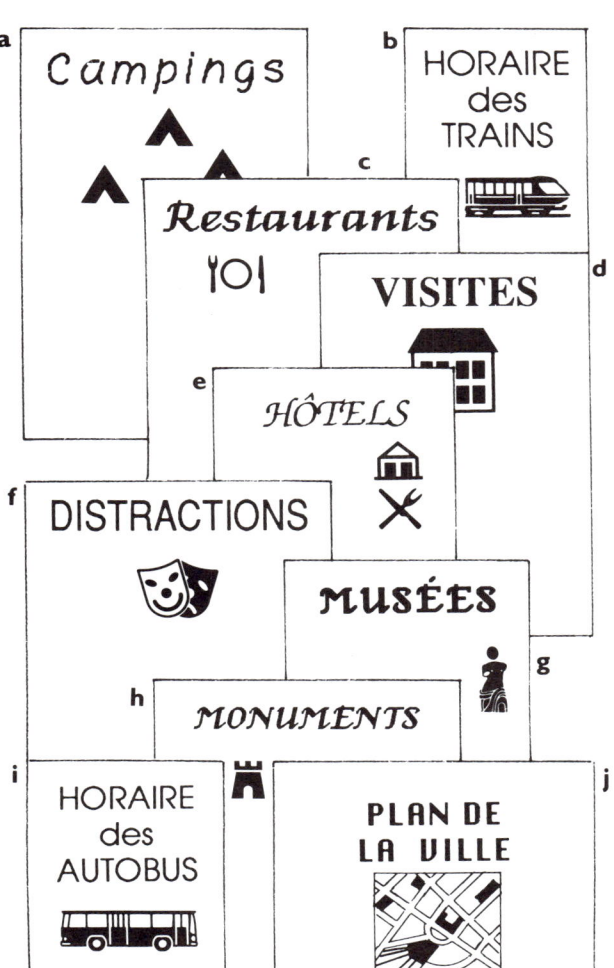

Information you need:

1. Somewhere to eat out
2. Somewhere to stay the night
3. Train times
4. A good campsite nearby
5. Interesting buildings to visit
6. How to find your way about
7. What museums to go to
8. Things to do
9. Day trips out of town
10. Bus times

C Read these notes. Then copy out the sentences below and fill in the gaps.

> Marc
> Tu peux aller au syndicat d'initiative? J'ai besoin d'un horaire des autobus de Bonville, et un horaire des trains pour aller à Nanterre. Merci.
> Pierre

> Louise
> Tu peux aller à l'office du tourisme? Je voudrais une liste des monuments et des distractions. Merci. Anne-Marie

1 Pierre wants a . . . and a . . .
2 Anne-Marie wants a list of . . . and a list of . . .

Writing

A Read this list of information you need while on holiday. Then copy and complete the notes below: write the French words you will look for on leaflets to get the information you need.

   Information you need:

   1 Somewhere to eat out
   2 Somewhere to stay the night
   3 Train times
   4 A good campsite nearby
   5 Interesting buildings to visit
   6 How to find your way about
   7 What museums to go to
   8 Things to do
   9 Day trips out of town
   10 Bus times

B Look at the notes in Reading task C. Change the key words and write them again to match these ideas instead.

   1 Ask Marc to go to the tourist office.
     Say you need a list of campsites and a town plan.
     Say thank you.
   2 Ask Louise to go to the tourist office.
     Say you'd like a train timetable and a list of museums.
     Say thank you.

Listening

A ▶ In this conversation six items are mentioned. Here they are, but in the wrong order. Write the numbers in the correct order, as you hear them. ◀

   1 List of tours   4 Bus timetable
   2 List of things to see 5 List of things to do
   3 Town plan   6 Train timetable

B ▶ Listen to these people asking for information leaflets.

   Write numbers 1–8. Look at the leaflets available and write the correct letter next to each number, to show what they are asking for. ◀

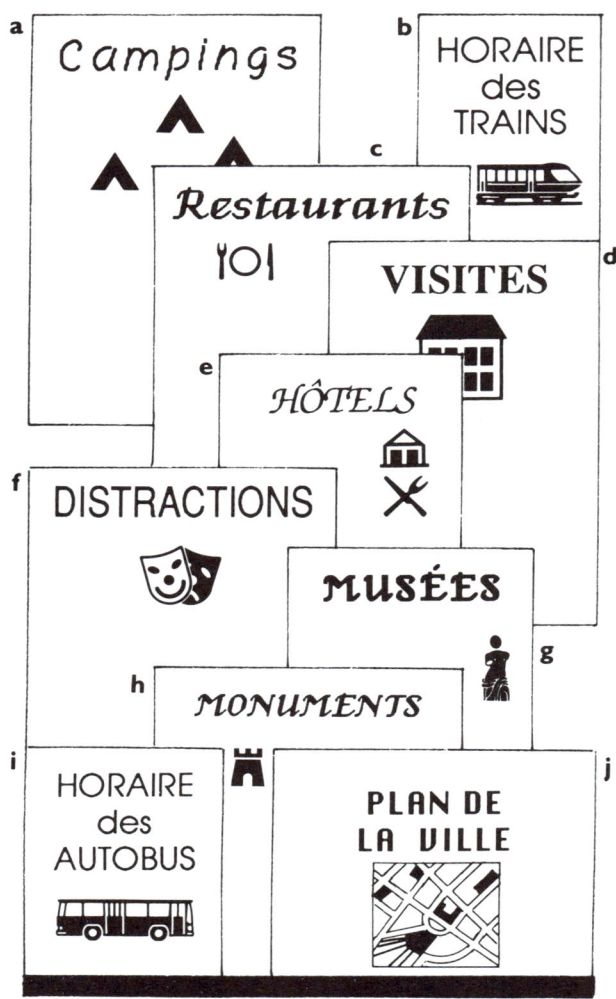

Speaking

A

You have heard people asking for information about these things. Try it yourself.

- For example, for the first one say *Un horaire des autobus, s'il vous plaît.*
- See if you can say them without looking at the word list.

B Work with a partner.
- Look at the list of information needed in Writing task A (page 44).
- Your partner is the official and starts off with *Bonjour, mademoiselle* or *Bonjour, monsieur.* You have to ask for the things you need.
- See how many you can do without looking at the word list.

▶ **To sum up . . .**

You should now be able to find a tourist office and get all the information you need.

Think about what you have done, and then fill in your record sheet.

▶12◀ At the petrol station

▶ **You will need these words:**

j'ai besoin . . .	I need . . .
d'une station-service	a petrol station
d'essence	petrol
d'huile	oil
d'eau	water
s'il vous plaît	please
merci	thank you
vingt litres de super	20 litres of 4-star
vingt litres d'essence sans plomb	20 litres of lead-free petrol
cent vingt francs	120 francs

Listening

A ▶ What are these eight people asking for?

Write in your book:

petrol station   petrol   oil   water

Listen to the tape, and write the number of each sentence under the correct word. ◀

B ▶ In this section six people are buying petrol.

Just listen to see if it is four-star petrol or lead-free petrol: *super* or *essence sans plomb*.

Write **1 – 6** in your book.

Listen to the tape, and write **** or LF next to each number. ◀

C ▶ Listen to these four conversations. Jot down as briefly as you can what is going on:

– what is being asked for (write **oil**, **petrol**, **water**)
– how many **litres** of petrol they are buying
– and if you can, **how much** they have to pay.

• Listen to each conversation twice, before you write anything down. ◀

Speaking

A The grid shows things you might need. Practise saying you need them: try to do it without looking at the words written under the pictures.

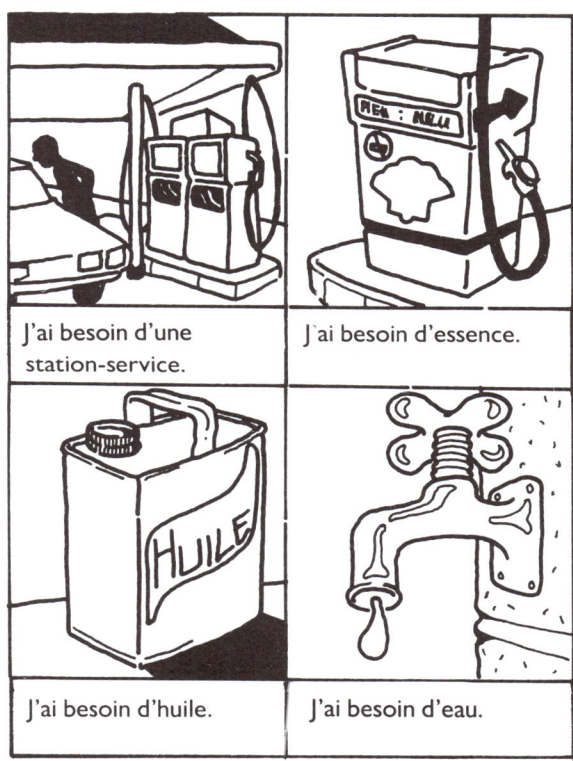

J'ai besoin d'une station-service.   J'ai besoin d'essence.

J'ai besoin d'huile.   J'ai besoin d'eau.

B • Fold a piece of paper into four.

• Copy the grid pictures, one in each section. Not the words, though.

• Cut or tear the paper into four along the folds.

• Get together with two or three others, put your picture 'cards' together in a pile between you, upside down.

• Take it in turns to pick a 'card' and say you need that item – *J'ai besoin d'* . . . .

• If you get it right, keep the card; if not, put it back at the bottom. See who gets the most cards.

C Get together with a partner. Act out these conversations, taking it in turns to play each part.

Then see if you can do one without the words in front of you; if you can, try the others too.

1 – Dix litres de super, s'il vous plaît.
   – Oui, madame.
   – Merci.
   – Soixante francs, s'il vous plaît. Merci, madame.

2 – J'ai besoin d'huile, s'il vous plaît.
   – Oui, monsieur. Vingt francs, s'il vous plaît.
   – Voilà. Merci.
   – Merci.

3 – Vingt litres d'essence sans plomb, s'il vous plaît.
   – Oui, monsieur.
   – Merci. C'est combien?
   – Cent dix francs, s'il vous plaît. Merci.

4 – J'ai besoin d'essence. Vingt litres de super, s'il vous plaît.
   – Oui, madame. C'est tout?
   – Euh non, j'ai besoin d'eau.
   – Voilà. Cent vingt francs, s'il vous plaît. Merci.

D With your partner, make up two new conversations.
- Say you need petrol or oil or water, or all three!
- Don't forget to say what kind of petrol you want, and how many litres.

Reading

A Look at these signs. What do they mean?

Write **1 – 6** in your book, and write the English word next to each number.

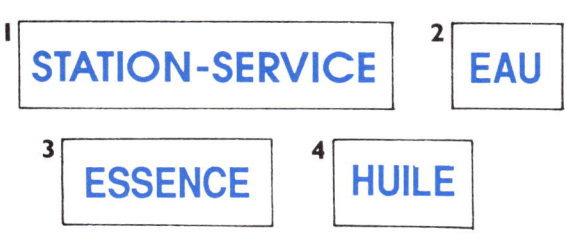

B You have bought some petrol from these four petrol pumps.

Write **1 – 4** in your book. Read the displays and write down how many litres of petrol you have bought, and how many francs it cost.

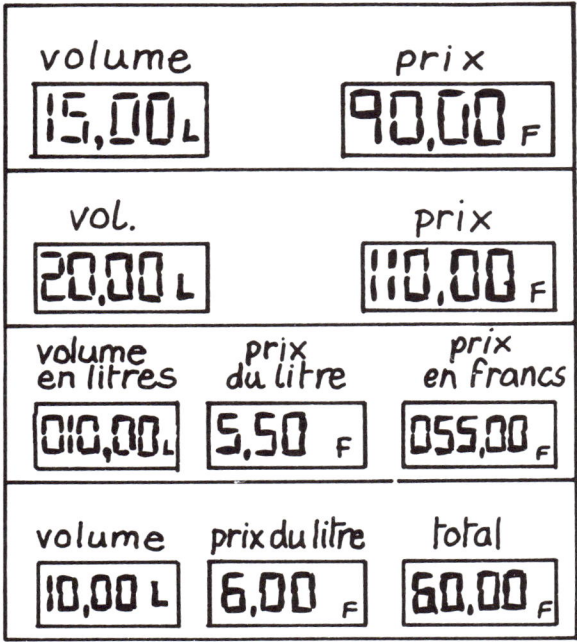

Writing

Write down the sentence you would use in each of these situations.

1. You need a petrol station.
2. You need some petrol.
3. You need some water.
4. You want 20 litres of four-star, please.
5. You say thank you.
6. You need some oil.
7. You want 20 litres of lead-free petrol.

▶ **Finally...**

You should now be able to buy what you need in a petrol station. 20 litres is about 4 ½ gallons. If you don't understand the price they ask for, read the numbers from the pump display or till.

Now fill in your record sheet.

≋13≋ Meeting people from other countries

Everyone enjoys talking about their home, or their holidays. Whether you're shopping for bread, queuing for the toilets at a campsite, or parked up with other lorry drivers to go through customs, one of the easiest ways to start talking to someone is to ask what country they come from.

▶ **Words you will need:**

où habitez-vous?	where do you live?
où exactement?	where exactly?
j'habite . . .	I live . . .
vous êtes allé . . . ?	
vous êtes allée . . . ?	have you been . . . ?
je suis allé . . .	
je suis allée . . .	I've been . . .
en	in/to (a country)
à	in/to (a town)
Grande-Bretagne	Great Britain
France	France
Suisse	Switzerland
Allemagne	Germany
Espagne	Spain
Italie	Italy
Belgique	Belgium

Note: use *allée* to refer to a woman or girl, *allé* to refer to a man or boy.

Listening

A Write numbers **1–7** in your book. ▶ Then listen to the tape: seven people mention a country from the list below. Write which country it is. You can use just the initials (but use Sp for Spain). ◀

Belgium
France
Germany
Great Britain
Italy
Spain
Switzerland

B ▶ Now listen again. Put a tick against the ones where the people say they live; and a cross against the ones they have been to. ◀

C ▶ Listen to these four conversations. You will hear people being asked where they live, and whether they have been to another country.

Copy the table below. Then, as you hear each conversation, write **1, 2** or **3** by each word to show what you heard first, second and last. ◀

Country lived in	Town lived in	Country visited
France	Paris	Italy
Britain	Southampton	Spain
Germany	Bonn	Switzerland
Belgium	Brussels	France

D ▶ Listen again carefully for the questions

Où habitez-vous?
Vous êtes allé . . .?
Où exactement?

and the answers

J'habite . . .
Je suis allé . . .

Don't write anything, just pick out the questions and answers. ◀

Speaking

A Where do you live?

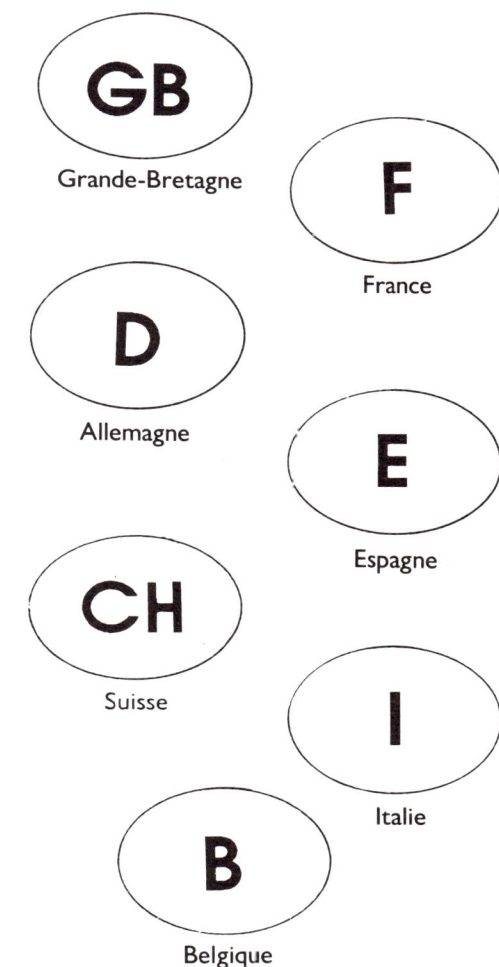

Work with a partner.

- One of you points to a badge and asks *Où habitez-vous?*
- The other has to reply *J'habite en . . .*, adding the correct French name.

B Have you been to . . .?
Do the same again. Point to a badge and ask a question. This time, the question is *Vous êtes allé en . . .?* and the answer is *Oui, je suis allé en . . .* (Or if you want to be awkward, you can just reply *Non!*)

C Now for a longer conversation. Ask the same two questions, but in between, find out **where exactly** your partner lives: *Où exactement?*

Take it in turns to ask: when you answer, use this table.

Où habitez-vous? J'habite en . . .	Où exactement? J'habite à . . .	Vous êtes allé en . . . ? Oui, je suis allé en . . . / Non!
France Grande-Bretagne Allemagne Belgique	Paris Southampton Bonn Bruxelles	Italie Espagne Suisse France

Reading

A
1
2
3
4

Read the French captions, and then complete the English ones:

1 Where . . . ?
 I live in . . .

2 . . . exactly?
 . . . in Birmingham.

3 Have you been to . . . ?
 Yes, . . . Madrid.

4 And have you been to . . . ?
 No!

B Can you find all seven countries from this unit in this wordsquare?

E	G	B	R	E	T	A	E	E
N	R	R	I	E	S	S	I	B
G	A	E	S	U	I	S	S	E
A	N	T	O	N	M	A	A	L
P	D	A	L	O	D	A	T	G
S	E	G	R	A	I	E	N	I
E	C	N	A	R	F	O	L	Q
E	S	E	I	L	A	T	I	U
A	L	L	E	M	A	G	N	E

C Tinkler Trading Ltd sent reps all over Europe. Read this report and then answer the questions.

```
Mme Wilson est allée en France, à Paris.
Elle y a passé une semaine. M. Walton a
passé une semaine en Espagne, à Barcelone,
et en Allemagne, à Berlin. Mme Gofton et
M. Holmes sont allés en Belgique, à
Bruxelles. M. Scoter est allé en Italie
et en Suisse. Mme Smith est restée en
Grande-Bretagne.
```

1 Who went to Spain?
2 Who went to Belgium?
3 Where did Mr Walton go?
4 Where did Mrs Wilson go?
5 Who went to Italy?
6 Who went to Switzerland?
7 What did Mrs Smith do?

Writing

A Complete the words:

1 Où hab_ _ _ _-vous?
2 Vo_ _ êt_ _ _ _lé en A_ _ _ _ _ _ _e?
3 J'h_ _ _ _ _ e_ G_ _ _ _ _-B_ _ _ _ _ _ _.
4 Où ex_ _ _ _ _ _ _ _?
5 Je s_ _ _ aL_ _ _ n E_ _ _ _ _ _.

B Here is some information about Madame Sollette:

> Madame Sollette lives in France, in Toulouse.
> She has been to Spain.
> She has been to Belgium.

Write out the four French questions you would need to ask her to get this information.

What if you don't wish to say you live in Great Britain?

If you prefer, learn one of these too:

- J'habite en Écosse
- J'habite en Irlande
- J'habite en Irlande du Nord
- J'habite au Pays de Galles
- J'habite en Angleterre

▶ **To sum up . . .**

You should be able to start up a conversation now. Starting is the hardest bit – so don't even think about what to say next!

Fill in your record sheet.

14 Breakfast

French breakfast is a treat. It may be supplied in your hotel or youth hostel, or you may buy your own food from a supermarket if you are camping or staying in a self-catering *gîte*.
You will probably not be offered cooked food, but instead, plenty of fresh French bread or croissants, and delicious coffee or hot chocolate (usually served in bowls!).
If breakfast is provided, there may be a menu, or just food laid out on the table; this unit will teach you to understand the menu and ask for what you want.

▶ Words you will need:

le petit déjeuner	breakfast	*du café*	coffee
du pain	bread	*du lait*	milk
des croissants	croissants (crescent-shaped pastries)	*du thé*	tea
		du chocolat	hot chocolate
des biscottes	biscottes (crisp mini-toasts)	*du sucre*	sugar
		du jus d'orange	orange juice
du beurre	butter		
de la confiture	jam	*avez-vous . . . ?*	have you got . . . ?
		s'il vous plaît	please

Listening

Use these pictures to do listening tasks A–E.

a le petit déjeuner	**b** du pain	**c** des croissants
d des biscottes	**e** du beurre	**f** de la confiture
g du café	**h** du lait	**i** du thé
j du chocolat	**k** du sucre	**l** du jus d'orange

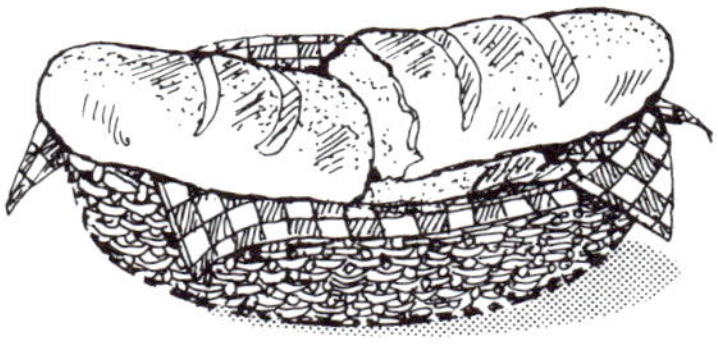

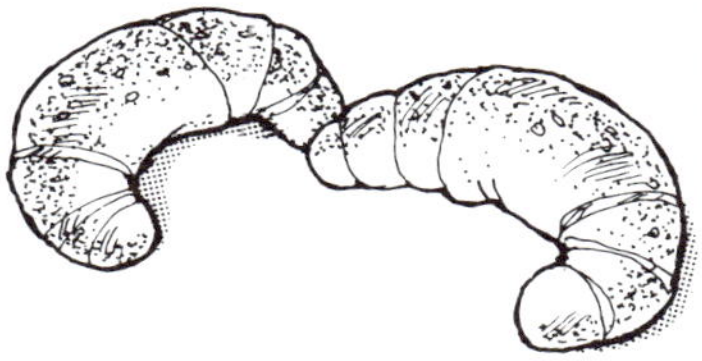

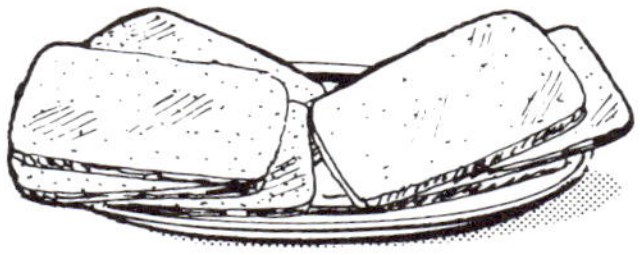

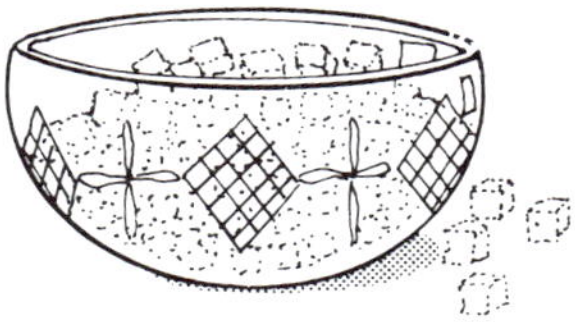

A ▶ You will hear names of some things you might eat for breakfast.
Write **1 – 6** in your book, and as you listen, put the correct letter from pictures **a – f** beside each number. ◀

B ▶ Now you will hear the words you need to order a drink. Write **1 – 6** and as you listen, choose the correct letters from pictures **g – l**. ◀

C ▶ When you order something, you can simply say its name and *s'il vous plaît*.
Or you can ask first whether they've got what you want: *Avez-vous . . . ?*

- Put **1 – 6** in your book.
- Listen to these six people ordering food.
- For each one, write down the correct letter from pictures **a – f** on page 55.
- Also, put **P** for 'please' or **?** for 'have you got . . . ?' ◀

D ▶ This is the same, only this time, they are ordering drinks.

- Put **1 – 6** in your book.
- For each one, write the correct letter from pictures **g – l**.
- Write also **P** for 'please' or **?** for 'have you got . . . ?'◀

E ▶ These three people are deciding what to have for breakfast.

- As you hear them talk to the waiter, listen for the food and drink they choose.
- Write down the letters from the pictures: each person will ask for five things. ◀

Speaking

A Look again at the pictures on page 55.

- Can you say in French what they are?
- Work with a partner. Take it in turns to choose a picture for your partner to name in French.

B Divide a piece of paper into 12. In each section draw or trace one of the pictures on page 55. Then play these card games.

1 For two or three people:
- Put the cards in a pile, face down, between you.
- Pick one up in turn, and say what it shows, in French.
- If you get it right, keep the card.
- If you get it wrong or don't know, put it back at the bottom.
- See who ends up with the most cards.

2 For three people:
- Share out all your cards.
- The aim is to collect all 12 pictures.
- When it is your turn, ask for something: *Avez-vous du café?* for example.
- The other player has to hand over that card if they have it. And you have to give them a card you don't want, in return.
- Keep going until one player has got a full set of all 12 pictures.

Keep your cards for later!

C Olivier, Suzanne and Paul are ordering their breakfast.

Practise ordering these breakfasts for yourself.

Then work with a partner.

- See if your partner can understand what you are asking for.
- Use your cards to check this: as you order your breakfast, your partner selects the cards you name and gives them to you.
- Then swap over.

D Now order your own breakfast.

Choose what you would like from page 55.

Your partner takes your order and has to give you the right cards to match what you ask for.

Reading

A These campers have to buy their breakfast from the supermarket. Here are their shopping lists.

Look back at the pictures on page 55, and for each shopping list, write the four matching letters.

B Look again at Olivier, Suzanne and Paul ordering their breakfast (on the left). For each one, write down the letters for the things they are ordering.

Writing

Using the pictures and shopping lists to help you, write out your own French breakfast menu. Choose at least five items.

▶ **Finally . . .**

You should now be able to understand a breakfast menu and order breakfast.

If you have to buy it, find a self-service shop, choose what you want, and read the price from the till.

Now fill in your record sheet.

◁15▷ Hiring something

Hiring something can be complicated. If you think you might want to hire a car, find out how the system works before you go. There are sometimes extra charges to pay: deposit, insurance, VAT.

Try to check what you're getting for your money! And make sure you ask for the *total* price. Ask to see the prices written down in the brochure – that will help too!

Catégories et Modèles		3 jours TTC	4 jours TTC	5 jours TTC	6 jours TTC
A Renault Supercinq	•	1095,70	1347,66	1597,66	1848,63
B Peugeot 205		1411,13	1667,97	1924,80	
C Renault 19	•	1843,75	2176,76		
D Peugeot 405		2346,68			
E Renault 25		2740,23			
F BMW 520 i. (ABS)		3340.82	40		
G Renault 21 GTX	•	2159,18	261		3535,16
H Renault 25 V6 AC	Automatique	3883,79	4679,	5473,63	6269,53
J Mercedes 190 AC		5105,47	6308,59	7516,60	8722,66
K Mercedes 300 AC		7319,34	8873,05	10426,76	11979,49

Europcar Location de voitures

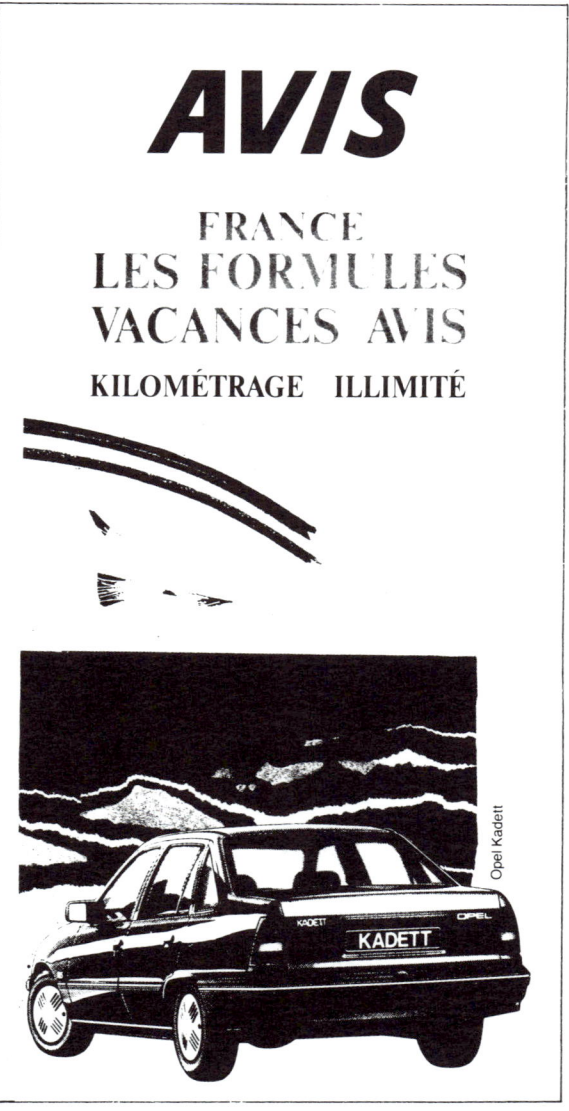

▶ Words you will need:

location de ...	... for hire
louer	to hire
une voiture	a car
un bateau	a boat
un vélo	a bike
c'est combien (en tout)?	how much is it altogether?
montrez-moi dans la brochure	show me in the brochure
voilà	there it is
par heure	for an hour
par jour	for a day
par semaine	for a week
ça va	that's fine, all right
ça ne va pas	that's no good

Listening

A ▶ You will hear people asking to hire something. Write numbers **1 – 5** in your book. Listen to the conversations, and find out what it is they want to hire. Write **car**, **boat** or **bike**. ◀

B ▶ Are they asking about hire by the hour, day or week? Listen again and write **H**, **D** or **W**. ◀

C ▶ In these conversations you have to find out if the person decides to hire, or not to. Write numbers **1 – 4**. Listen and put a tick for yes, a cross for no. ◀

Speaking

A

Can you ask how much it costs to hire these items? Ask the question in two parts:

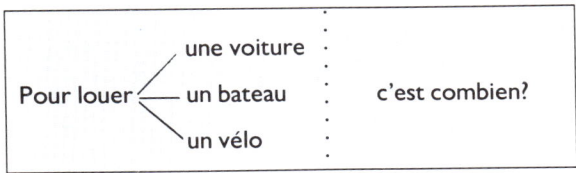

Work with a partner. Ask them to point to the thing you want to hire, to show they can understand.

B Now say how long you want to hire it for.

Work with a partner again: see if they can point to the right picture.

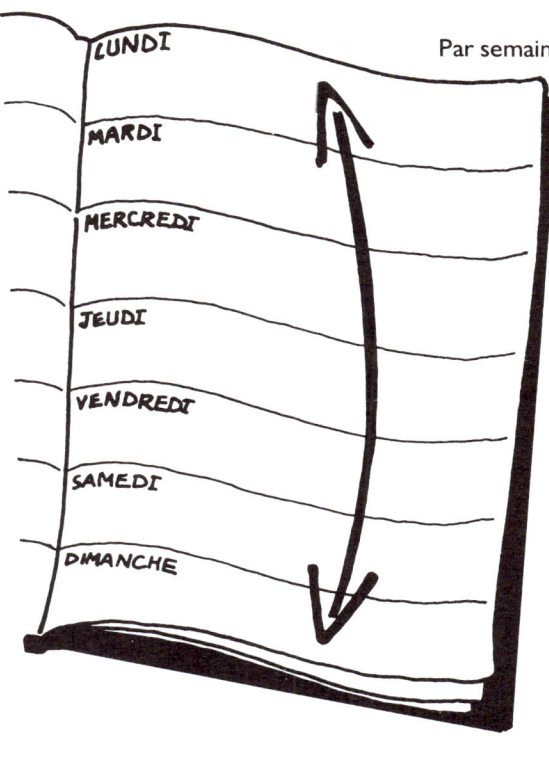

Par semaine

Par jour

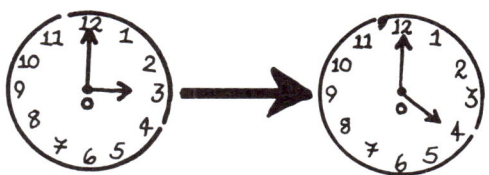

Par heure

C Read this scene with your partner. Act it out.

Practise until you can say it in French while looking only at the English captions below.

1

— How much is it to hire a car?

2

— For a day? Or for a week?
— For a week.

3

— There it is, in the brochure.
— Show me, please.

4

— Is that all right?
— No, that's no good.

Reading

Look at these signs and complete the sentences which follow.

1
LOCATION de BATEAUX!!
20 F par heure
100 F par jour

2
Vélos à louer
25 F par heure
60 F par jour

3
LOCATION de VOITURES
Par semaine : 2000 F en tout
Par jour : 300 F en tout

4
CARAVANES à LOUER
1000 F par semaine

a To hire a boat costs . . . francs per hour and . . . francs per day.
b To hire a . . . costs 25 francs for an hour.
c To hire a . . . costs 300 francs a day.
d The car rental *is/is not* the total cost.
e To hire a car costs . . . for a day, and . . . for a week.
f To hire a caravan costs 1 000 francs for a . . .

Writing

A Write out your own adverts in French for these rental companies.

1 Car hire
  250 francs a day
  1 250 francs a week

2 Bikes for hire
  50 francs a day
  20 francs an hour

3 To hire – boats
  50 francs an hour
  250 francs a day

B Copy out this conversation, changing the English words into French.

— Je voudrais to hire une voiture.

— A car? Mais oui!

— How much is it en tout?

— There it is, dans la brochure.

— Par semaine ou for a day?

— For a week! Ça va?

— Oui oui, that's fine!

▶ **And finally . . .**

You should be able to manage with hiring now. If you're not sure you've understood the price, ask to see it in writing!

NB. VAT in French is TVA (it stands for *Taxe à la Valeur Ajoutée*).

Now fill in your record sheet.

⋛16⋚ Going by bus

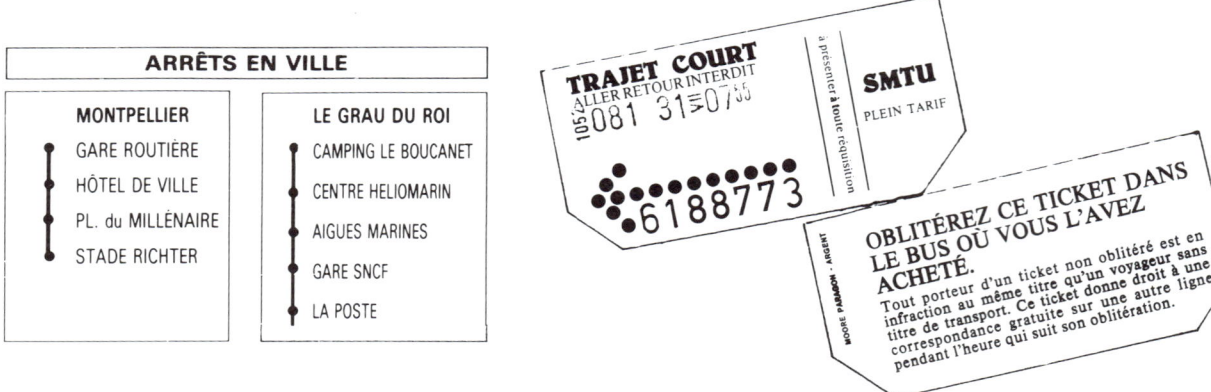

ARRÊTS EN VILLE	
MONTPELLIER	**LE GRAU DU ROI**
• GARE ROUTIÈRE	• CAMPING LE BOUCANET
• HÔTEL DE VILLE	• CENTRE HELIOMARIN
• PL. du MILLÉNAIRE	• AIGUES MARINES
• STADE RICHTER	• GARE SNCF
	• LA POSTE

▶ **Words you will need:**

un autobus	a bus	le camping	the campsite
un arrêt	a bus stop	la gare	the station
un billet	a ticket	la gare routière	the bus station
		le port	the harbour
un aller simple pour . . .	one single to . . .	voilà	here it is
		merci	thank you
un aller-retour pour . . .	one return to . . .	s'il vous plaît	please
deux allers simples pour . . .	two singles to . . .		
deux aller-retour pour . . .	two returns to . . .		

In Paris, you use the same tickets on buses as you do on the métro. Buy them from tobacconists, bus drivers or métro stations. You may need one, two or more for a journey; and you have to stamp them in a machine on the bus. But it's faster to go by métro, and cheaper, as you only need one ticket per journey.

Outside towns, a bus or coach is usually called a *car* instead. You buy a ticket from the driver as you get on. If you don't understand the price, look at the driver's ticket machine.

Listening

A Look at these pictures.

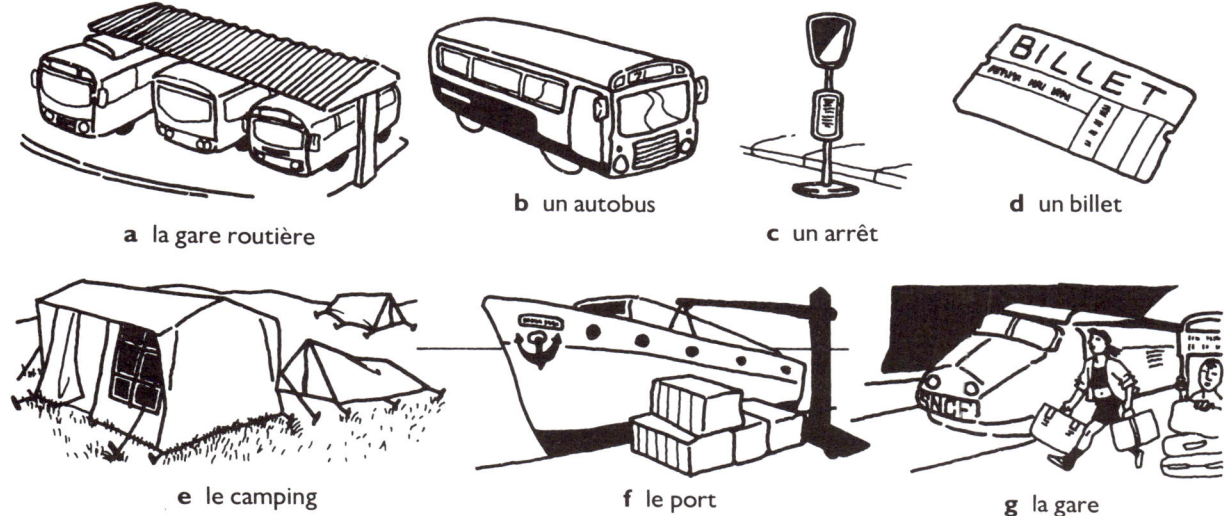

a la gare routière
b un autobus
c un arrêt
d un billet
e le camping
f le port
g la gare

▶ Write **1–7** in your book. Listen to the tape, and write the correct letter from the pictures next to each number. ◀

B ▶ This time you will hear the words in sentences. Just listen for the sounds you know. Write **1–7** again, and use the pictures and letters above. ◀

C ▶ Now you will hear four people asking for tickets.

- In each sentence, listen for two things
  – do they want one or two tickets?
  – do they want singles or returns?
- Write **1–4** in your book.
- For each sentence, write **1** or **2**, and **S** for single, **R** for return. ◀

D ▶ Here are six more passengers. This time, listen for the place they want to go to. Look at the pictures on the right. Write **1–6** in your book, and choose the right letter for each number. ◀

E ▶ What tickets are these people buying?

Copy the grid into your book.

As you listen to the tape, tick the right columns to show what tickets they buy and how many. ◀

	1	2	Single	Return	Port	Campsite	Station	Bus station
1								
2								
3								
4								
5								
6								
7								
8								

Speaking

A Look at the pictures you used in Listening task A on page 63.

- See if you can say what they are, in French.
- Try it with the French words covered up.
- Work with a partner. Take it in turns to say the French words; can your partner point to the right picture?

B

un	aller simple aller-retour	pour	le camping le port la gare la gare routière Lille Grasse	s'il vous plaît
deux	allers simples aller-retour			

Now buy a ticket. First, practise the different tickets to ask for by yourself. Make up four different sentences using the words in the grid above.

C • Now work with a partner.

Ask for one or two tickets to somewhere, as you have just been doing in task B.

- Your partner replies *Voilà*, and you reply *Merci*.
- Then swap over.
- Can you and your partner understand each other? Use the pictures in Listening task D to find out: when one of you asks for a ticket, the other points to the right picture.

Reading

A Choose the right answer to each question. Just write the number and the correct letter, **a**, **b** or **c**.

1 When you arrive in France by boat, you will find yourself in:
  a un billet
  b le port
  c la gare

2 If you want to catch a bus on the street, you look for:
  a un arrêt
  b le camping
  c un aller simple

3 Your train arrives at:
  a la gare routière
  b un arrêt
  c la gare

4 A bus in a French town is called:
  a un autobus
  b le port
  c un aller-retour

5 Your bus will stop here last of all:
  a la gare
  b la gare routière
  c le camping

6 If you want a ticket, you might ask for:
  a un arrêt
  b un autobus
  c un aller simple

7 If you are using a tent for your holiday, you will need to find:
  a un camping
  b une gare
  c un billet

B Six people are asking for tickets, using these words:

  a Deux allers simples pour le camping, s'il vous plaît.
  b Deux aller-retour pour Grasse, s'il vous plaît.
  c Un aller-retour pour le port, s'il vous plaît.
  d Un aller simple pour la gare, s'il vous plaît.
  e Deux allers simples pour la gare routière, s'il vous plaît.
  f Un aller simple pour le port, s'il vous plaît.

Answer these by writing the correct letter next to each number.

Which person is asking for:

1 a single to the station?
2 a single to the port?
3 two returns to Grasse?
4 two singles to the campsite?
5 two singles to the bus station?
6 a return to the port?

Writing

A Find in this box the French words for

  campsite
  bus station
  harbour

Use each of the letters once only. Which five letters are not used?

A	A	C	C	E	È	E	E	G	G
	I	I	M	M	N	N	O	O	
P	P	R	R	R	R	T	T	U	U

Now use the letters in this box once only, to make the French for

  bus
  bus stop
  ticket

Which four letters are not used?

A	A	B	B	Ê	E	I	I
	L	L	O	O	R	R	
S	S	T	T	T	T	U	U

B These sentences are muddled. Write them out with the words in the proper order.

1 aller-retour Deux le camping, pour s'il vous plaît.
2 Un simple aller pour port, le s'il vous plaît.
3 la gare, aller-retour Un pour s'il vous plaît.
4 pour la gare routière, simples Deux allers s'il vous plaît.

 And to sum up . . .

You should be able to find a bus stop or bus station and buy the tickets you want.

Now fill in your record sheet.

17 Lost property

Although it is hard to get lost property back, you will probably want to claim the money from insurance. To do that you will have to inform someone official as soon as you can – the hotel *Réception*, a lost property office or the police.

▶ **Words you will need:**

le bureau des objets trouvés	lost property office
la gendarmerie	police station
j'ai perdu . . .	I've lost . . .
de l'argent	some money
mon passeport	my passport
une valise	a suitcase
un sac	a bag
où l'avez-vous laissé?	where did you leave it?
je l'ai laissé . . .	I left it . . .
dans la rue	in the street
à la gare	at the station
à l'hôtel	at the hotel
dans ma chambre	in my room
c'est comment?	what is it like?
ça vaut combien?	what is it worth?
votre nom et votre adresse?	your name and address?

Listening

A ▶ Listen to these eight people saying what they have lost. Match the number on the tape with the letter of the picture. ◀

B The official will probably ask these questions:

  a Where did you leave it?
  b What is it like?
  c What is it worth?
  d What is your name and address?

▶ Write 1 – 7. Listen to the questions, and write the correct letter, **a – d**, next to the numbers. ◀

C ▶ These people are saying where they left something. Copy these English words, then write the number of each sentence next to the right ones as you listen. ◀

street
station
hotel
room

D ▶ Now listen to three conversations. For each one, answer three questions:

  a What was lost?
  b Where was it lost?
  c What is the last question the official asks?

Write your answers in notes. ◀

Speaking

A The pictures in Listening task A show items you have lost.

- Practise saying that you've lost each of them: *J'ai perdu . . .*

- Work with a partner: they point to the correct picture to show they understand. Then swap over.

B Now say where you left it: *Je l'ai laissé . . .* Use the pictures below.

- Your partner asks where you left it: *Où l'avez vous laissé?*

- When you answer, they point to the right picture. Then swap over.

C Act this conversation with your partner. Take turns to be the hotel guest and the receptionist. Then cover up the French captions and see how many you can do looking only at the pictures.

— J'ai perdu un sac!
— Où l'avez-vous laissé?

— À la gare?
  Dans la rue?
— Non! À l'hôtel...
  Dans ma chambre!

— C'est comment?
  Ça vaut combien?

— Votre nom et votre adresse, s'il vous plaît.

Reading

A You've lost something and want to report it. Which of these signs might you look for? Write the correct letters.

a POSTE b RÉCEPTION c PÂTISSERIE d GENDARMERIE
e STATION-SERVICE f BUREAU DES OBJETS TROUVÉS g DOUANE

B Read this letter to a hotel. Then copy and complete the sentences which follow.

> Lyon, le 25 février
>
> Monsieur/Madame
>
> J'ai perdu un sac à l'hôtel, le 21 février. Je l'ai laissé dans ma chambre, numéro 361. Il est noir et il vaut 100 Francs. Mon nom et mon adresse sont:
>
> Marc Choupon
> 10 place Rouville
> 69 001 LYON
>
> Merci.   Marc Choupon

1 Marc lost a . . . at the . . . .
2 He left it in his . . . .
3 It was room number . . . .
4 It was on the . . . of February.
5 It is black, and worth . . . .

C Read this newspaper advertisement and complete the sentences below.

> **Perdus!!**
>
> Le 4 octobre, à Chamonix
> À la gare ou dans la rue
> une valise, un sac et mon passeport
>
> **Au secours!!**
>
> Tél. 23.03.11.18

1 A . . . and a . . . and a . . . were lost.
2 They were lost at . . . or in . . . .
3 You should contact the owner by . . . .

Writing

A Take out six letters from each, and these will become French questions you have learned in this unit.

Write them out correctly.

1 Oùt sl'averz-vours claistsé?
2 Sça vadwuti combopien?
3 Gvotre snome et vgeotre madresse?
4 C'esty scoomtimenty?

B Leave a note for your friend.
- Say you have lost your passport.
- Say you lost it at the station.

C Write a letter to a hotel. Use Reading task B to help you.
- Say you have lost a bag.
- Say you left it at the hotel, in your room.
- Say it is worth 250 francs.
- Give your name and address.

▶ To sum up . . .

You should now be able to inform someone what you have lost and where.
Then you can claim the insurance money, or if you're lucky you'll get it back!

Now fill in your record sheet.

18 Telling the time

Le train à vapeur des Cévennes

▶ Words you will need:

quelle heure est-il?	what time is it?	à quelle heure est . . .?	what time is. . .?
il est une heure	it's one o'clock	à une heure	at one o'clock
il est deux heures	it's two o'clock		
il est deux heures moins le quart	it's quarter to two	une, deux,	1 2
il est deux heures et quart	it's quarter past two	trois, quatre,	3 4
		cinq, six,	5 6
il est deux heures et demie	it's half past two	sept, huit,	7 8
		neuf, dix,	9 10
il est midi	it's midday	onze	11
il est minuit	it's midnight		

Listening

A ► You will hear six times. Listen for the numbers, and write them down. ◄

B ► Listen, especially for the minute hand. Look at the clock faces and write down the letters in the correct order as you hear the times. ◄

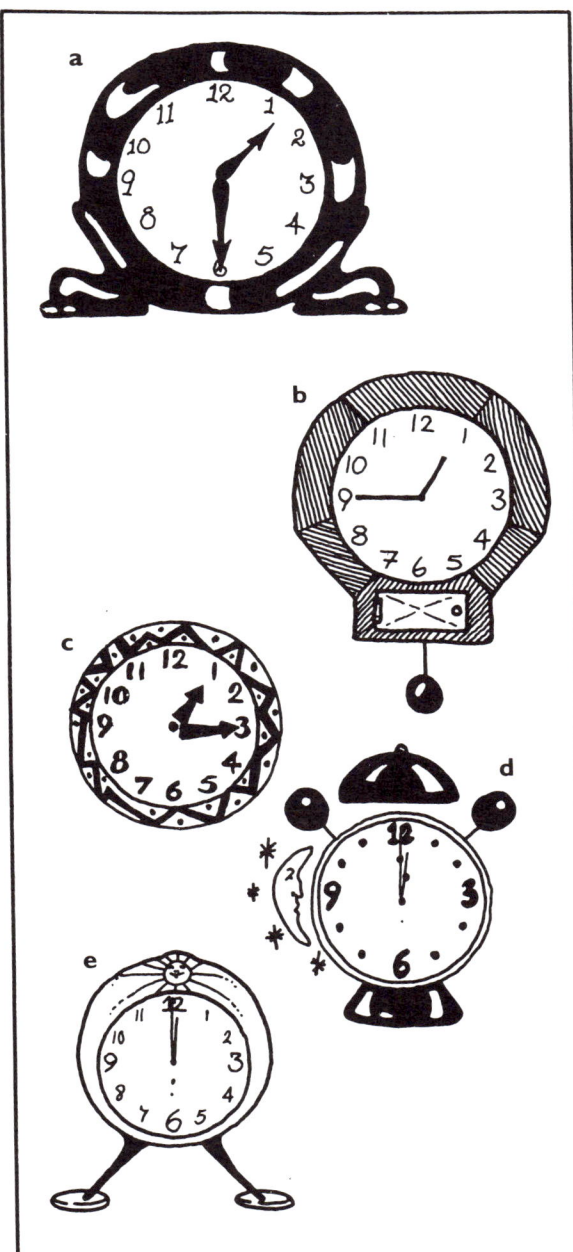

C Write these words in your book:

disco
match
train
film
café
cinema

► Now listen to the tape, to find out at what time these things are happening.

Write the correct time next to or under each event. ◄

Write it the easiest, shortest way you can, in numbers,
like this: **8.45, 4.15**

or like this: **¼ to 9, ¼ past 4**

D ► Now see if you can do these. Just write down the times, as easily as you can. ◄

Speaking

A Look at these clocks. Cover the French words, and practise saying the time aloud in French. Check each one to see if you are right.

Then work with a partner.

- Take it in turns to ask *Quelle heure est-il?*
- The other one answers, in French, from the clocks.
- Test each other on all of them.

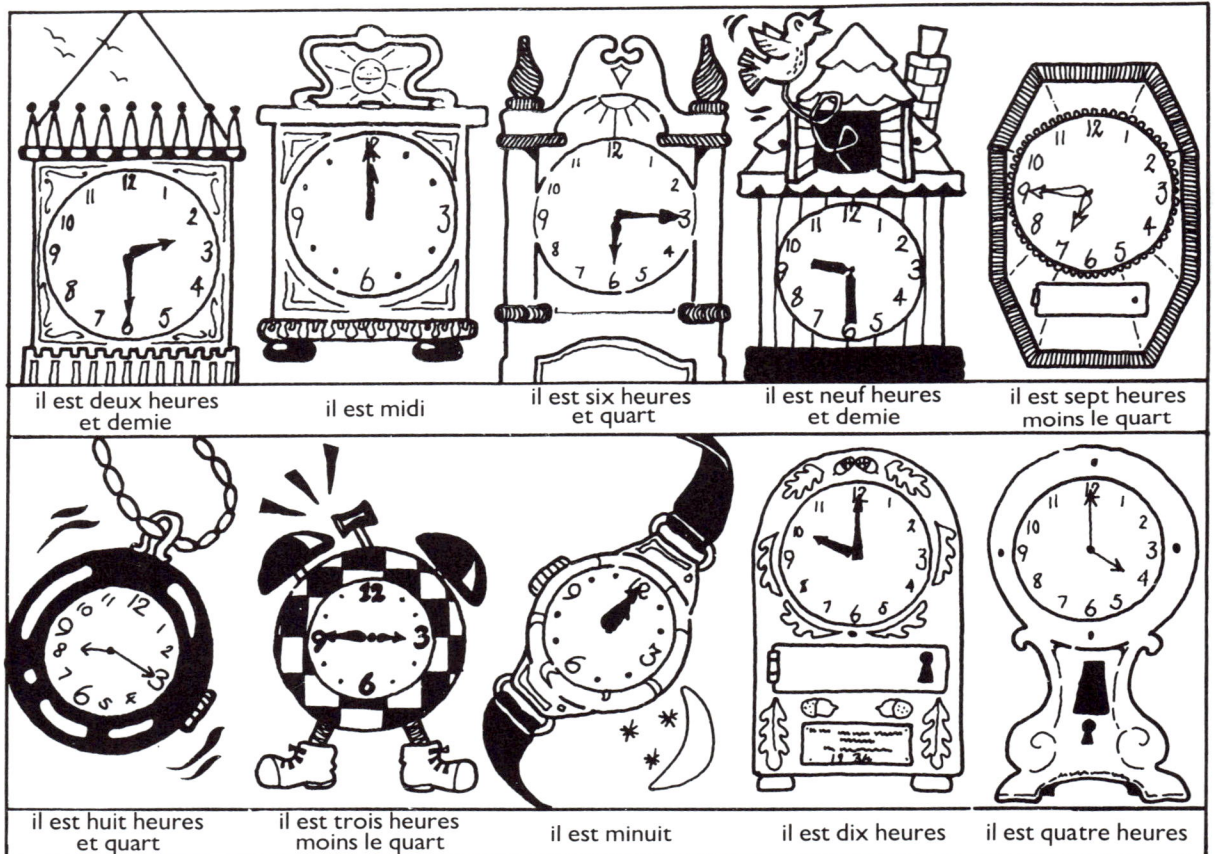

il est deux heures et demie

il est midi

il est six heures et quart

il est neuf heures et demie

il est sept heures moins le quart

il est huit heures et quart

il est trois heures moins le quart

il est minuit

il est dix heures

il est quatre heures

B Decide for yourself what time the events in this list are at; write the times in your book. Then find a partner.

- Your partner asks you in French what time one of the events starts; give them the information.

Then move on to another event. Do all of them.

- Then start again: now it's your turn to ask the questions and find out from your partner what time the events are on.

À quelle heure est la fête?	À _____ heures _____
le match?	
le train?	
le film?	
le concert?	

Reading

Read these diary notes. At what time are all these things happening? Just write the time, in figures.

mercredi 16	Chez Alain, à huit heures. Cinéma, avec Jules et Jim, à six heures et quart. Café René, Place des Cigales, à une heure et demie. Fête, chez Jeanne, à dix heures moins le quart. Midi, chez moi : déjeuner avec Sophie.

Writing

A Look at these clocks. Write down, in words, the time each one shows.
So the first one will be *Il est cinq heures*.

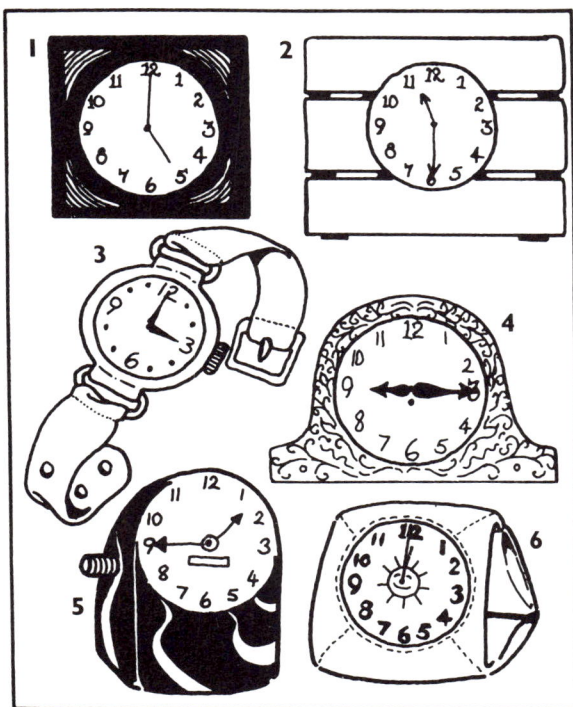

B Your friend wants to see you. But you already have a busy day planned! Leave a note, in French, listing your appointments.

> Café, half past eight.
> Jardin des Plantes, eleven o'clock.
> Restaurant du Coin, midday.
> Match, quarter past two.
> Film, quarter to six.
> Discothèque, midnight.

▶ And finally . . .

You should now be able to tell the time in French.

Now fill in your record sheet.

By the way, what do the French eat for breakfast?
Huit heures bix, of course!

19 Booking at a hotel

You can book package holidays to France at your travel agent's. But you might hear of a really good hotel and want to book for yourself. Perhaps you want to tour France and find a new hotel every night! Hotels are graded like British hotels, one-star to four-stars.

▶ **Words you will need:**

je voudrais	I would like	*pour une nuit*	for one night
une chambre	a room	*pour deux nuits*	for two nights
deux chambres	two rooms	*à partir du 3 avril*	from the 3rd of April
une chambre à un lit	a single room (with one bed)		
une chambre à deux lits	a double room (with two beds)	and the other holiday months:	
		mai *juin* *juillet*	
avec douche	with a shower	May June July	
avec WC	with a toilet	*août* *septembre* *octobre*	
		August September October	

Reading

A Read this letter to a hotel in France, then answer the questions.

```
                Netherton, le 5 avril
Monsieur/Madame
Je voudrais réserver une chambre
à un lit, avec douche et WC,
pour trois nuits, à partir
du 4 août.
   Merci,   Gillian Blackett.
```

1 When did Gillian write the letter?
2 How many rooms does she want?
3 What does she want in the room?
4 How long does she plan to stay?
5 What date will she arrive?

B A friend has brought you this advert for a hotel in France.

> **Hôtel de la Plage**
> **L'Hôtel de la Plage est idéal!**
> Nous avons 30 chambres:
> – 10 chambres avec douche, 20 chambres avec douche et WC
> – 12 chambres à un lit, 18 chambres à deux lits
> Nous sommes ouverts du 1 avril au 31 octobre.
>
> **Bienvenue à l'Hôtel de la Plage!**
> *Adresse:* 21, rue de la Plage, Menton

Copy this out and fill in the gaps:

This hotel is in a town called . . . .

There are . . . rooms with a shower and no toilet.

. . . rooms have both shower and toilet.

There are . . . single rooms and . . . double rooms.

The hotel is open from . . . until . . . .

The address to write to is:

Hôtel de la Plage
. . . .
. . . .
France

Writing

A Use the letter from Gillian Blackett in Reading task A to help you write some more letters, using the details below. Start with *Monsieur/Madame,* then add on each phrase, changing the details. Leave out anything you don't need.

	How many rooms	Type of room	Nights	Date	Shower	Toilet
1	1	single	2	30 May	✓	
2	1	double	3	14 July		
3	1	double	1	16 June	✓	✓
4	2	singles	4	17 September	✓	✓
5	1 / 2	double and singles	7	18 August		

B You're working in a seaside hotel in Britain one summer. The owners ask you to write an advert for their hotel, to go in a French brochure.

Look at the advert in Reading task B. See if you can change it to match this hotel:

> **Seaview Hotel**
> Rooms: 24
> Rooms with shower: 20
> Rooms with shower and toilet: 4
> Single rooms: 12
> Double rooms: 12
>
> *Open from 1st April to 31 October*

Listening

You are waiting in a long queue at a hotel.

A ▶ Listen to four people in front of you asking for rooms.

- Write how many rooms they want, and for how many nights. ◀
- Write it in your book like this:

	Rooms	Nights
1	2	1
2		

B ▶ Now write numbers **1 – 6**.
- Listen to the tape; do these people want rooms with two beds or one bed?
- Write **2** or **1** for each one. ◀

C ▶ Listen to the tape for B again.
- Find out which ones want a shower or toilet as well.
- Write **S** for shower, **T** for toilet. ◀

D ▶ Listen to the questions the hotel owner asks. The pictures show the questions, but in the wrong order. Write down the letters from the pictures in the correct order as you hear them. ◀

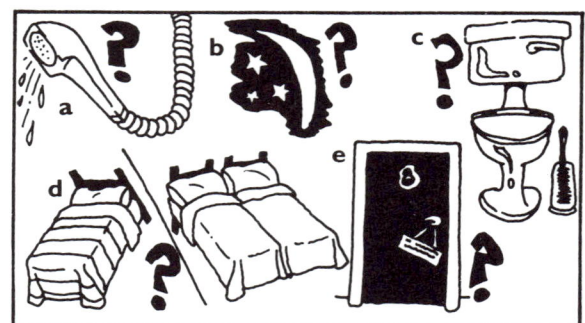

Speaking

A

– Je voudrais une chambre, s'il vous plaît.

– Pour une nuit?
– Non, pour deux nuits.

— Une chambre à un lit?
— Non, à deux lits, s'il vous plaît.

— Avec douche?
— Oui, et avec WC.

— Eh bien . . . une chambre . . .
à deux lits . . . avec douche
et WC . . . pour deux nuits . . .
c'est la chambre 12.

Look at the pictures; say the French sentences. Cover up the French captions: can you still say the sentences, looking only at the pictures?

Next, can you learn to say them while looking at these English sentences instead?
1 I'd like a room please.
2 For one night?
  No, for two nights.
3 A single room?
  No, a double, please.
4 With a shower?
  Yes, and with a toilet.
(And lastly, the hard one!!)
5 Right . . . one room . . . double . . . with shower and toilet . . . for two nights . . . that's room 12.

B How many of these rooms can you ask for in French?

	Rooms	Beds	Nights	Shower	Toilet
1	1	1	1		
2	1	2	1	✓	
3	2	2	3	✓	✓
4	2	1	2	✓	✓
5	1	2	1		

Remember, the main thing is to ask for a room:
Je voudrais une chambre, s'il vous plaît.
Then say the rest, a bit at a time!

C Work with a partner.

- Write out a new grid of rooms to ask for, like the one in task B. Fill in the numbers yourself.
- Your partner draws an empty grid – just the columns with headings.
- Ask for your rooms, one after the other. Your partner listens and fills in the details in his/her grid.
- When you've finished, compare your grids: are they the same?
- Then swap over!

▶ **Finally . . .**

You should be able to write to a hotel and book a room, or book in when you arrive.

Think about what you have done, and then fill in your record sheet.

20 On the métro in Paris

This unit will help you use the métro to get around in Paris. The métro is fast, clean and cheap. You buy one ticket, at 5 francs, for one journey, however long. You can buy tickets from tobacconists, or in stations. You can save money by buying a *carnet* – a book of ten tickets.

You can also buy a travel card to use as many times as you want on the same day or over three or five days. These are useful if you want to see a lot of the city.

▶ **Words you will need:**

un ticket s'il vous plaît	one ticket, please	TABAC	tobacconist
deux tickets, s'il vous plaît	two tickets, please	MÉTRO	métro (underground train)
un carnet, s'il vous plaît	a book of tickets, please	BILLETS	tickets
		ENTRÉE	entrance
		SORTIE	exit
cinq francs, s'il vous plaît	five francs, please	CORRESPONDANCE	connection (for changing trains)
dix francs, s'il vous plaît	ten francs, please		
trente francs, s'il vous plaît	thirty francs, please	DIRECTION . . .	direction . . . (. . . Line – the final station in the right direction tells you the name of the line)

Listening

A You will need to be able to recognise these words when using the métro.
▶ Write **1 – 7** in your book. Listen to the tape and look at the words below; as you hear a word write the correct letter next to each number. ◀

- **A** DIRECTION
- **B** MÉTRO
- **C** TICKETS
- **D** ENTRANCE
- **E** EXIT
- **F** TOBACCONIST
- **G** CONNECTION

B ▶ Now you will hear the same words in sentences. Write **1 – 7** again, and use the same letters as you did in Task A. ◀

C ▶ You will hear someone asking for a ticket or being told how much it costs. Write **1 – 6** in your book, and put the correct letter from the pictures below, next to each number. ◀

D ▶ Here are three conversations. Listen to the tape, look at pictures a – f again, and write two letters for each conversation: one for the tickets, one for the price. ◀

Speaking

– Un carnet, s'il vous plaît.
– Trente francs, s'il vous plaît.

– Un ticket, s'il vous plaît.
– Cinq francs, s'il vous plaît.

– Deux tickets, s'il vous plaît.
– Dix francs, s'il vous plaît.

Now it's up to you to buy tickets. Work with a partner.

- Choose one of the three boxes; ask for whatever is in it.
- Your partner has to tell you the right price.
- Then it's his/her turn to ask, and your turn to say the price.
- Carry on until you've both had six turns at buying tickets.

Reading and writing

A You might need to spot these signs:

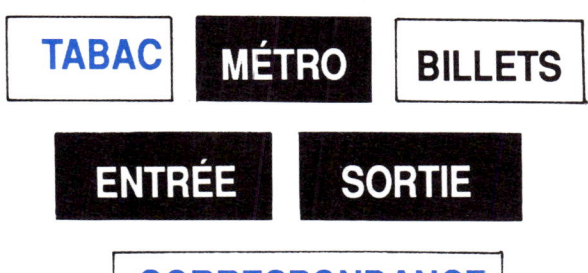

Copy the sign which answers each of these questions.

1. You want the way in.
2. You want to buy tickets in the station.
3. You need Direction Balard.
4. You want the way out.
5. You are changing trains at a station.
6. You are in the street, looking for a tobacconist.
7. You are in the street, looking for a métro station.

B Using a métro map.

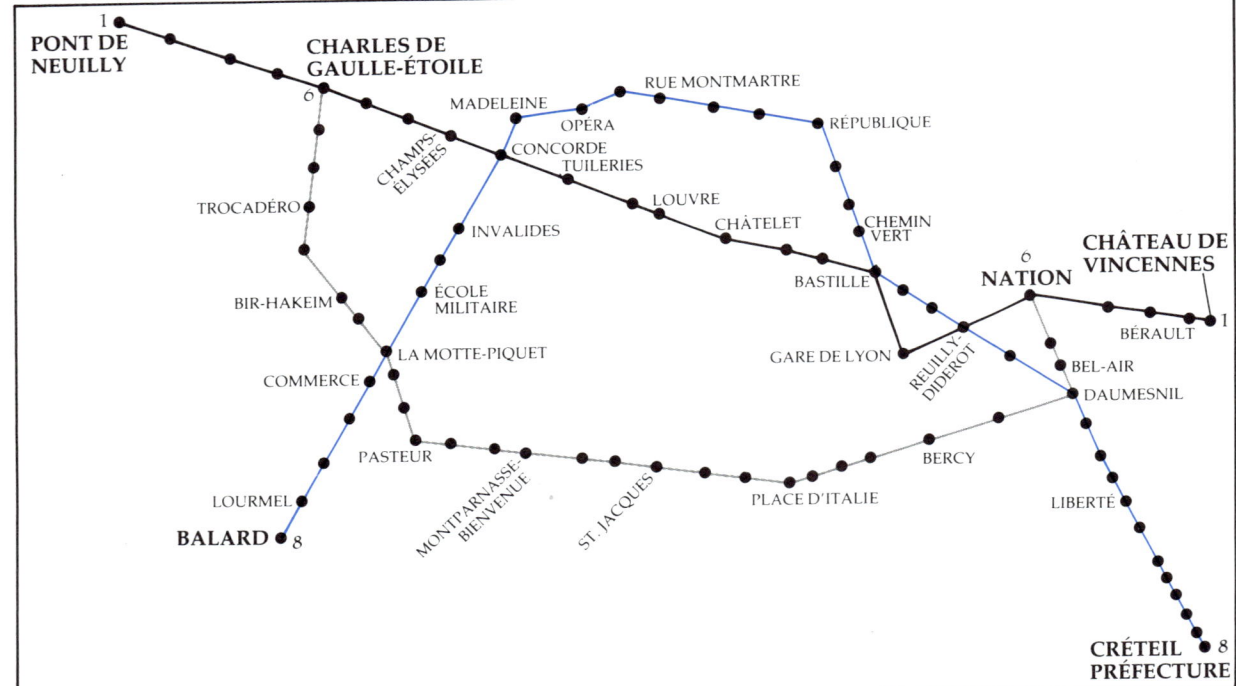

You will find a métro map at stations, inside and out, in leaflets you can pick up at tourist information points, and in guide books.

This map shows just a small part of the system (there's a complete map on page 81).

Here's how to use it.

1 Find the station you are starting from.
2 Find the station you are going to.
3 Look along the coloured line in that direction until you reach the end.
4 The last station on that line is the DIRECTION you must look for.
5 Follow the signs for that DIRECTION in the station: they will take you to the right platform.
6 Get on the first train that arrives. Watch for your stop: it helps if you count the number of stops before yours, so that you are ready to get off.

Here's an example.

You start at OPÉRA: you are going to RÉPUBLIQUE: so you need to follow DIRECTION CRÉTEIL PRÉFECTURE.

Use the map to work out which DIRECTION you need for these journeys. Copy out the sentence and fill in the name.

1 You start at OPÉRA. You are going to INVALIDES, so follow DIRECTION . . . .
2 You start at ST JACQUES. You are going to BERCY, so follow DIRECTION . . . .
3 You are at PASTEUR and want to go to TROCADÉRO. Follow DIRECTION . . . .
4 You are at CONCORDE and want to go to CHAMPS-ÉLYSÉES. Follow DIRECTION . . . .
5 You start at CONCORDE. You are going to GARE DE LYON. Follow DIRECTION . . . .

Make up three journeys of your own, between any two stations on one coloured line.

C You may have to change trains and change lines, to get to where you want to go. Here's how you do it.

1 Look for a station which is on the line you start on and also on the line your stop is on.
2 Find the Direction to get to that station, and get off there.

3 Now check the new Direction of the stop you want to end up at.
4 Head for the CORRESPONDANCE sign to change lines.
5 Follow the signs to the platform for your second train and travel to the stop you wanted.

For example:

You are at MADELEINE: you want to go to LOUVRE.
First take DIRECTION BALARD, change at CONCORDE. Now take DIRECTION CHÂTEAU DE VINCENNES and you will get to LOUVRE.

Can you work out how to get to these places, with a change of line?
Copy out the journeys, filling in the gaps.

1 You start at TROCADÉRO: you want INVALIDES.
First take DIRECTION NATION, change at . . . . Now take DIRECTION . . . .

2 Start at RÉPUBLIQUE: go to GARE DE LYON.
First take DIRECTION . . . and change at BASTILLE. Now take DIRECTION . . . .

D Work with a partner or on your own.

- Make up journeys for yourself, or for your partner to find on the map.
- Choose a starting point, and a stopping point.
- Work out how to get there!

> ▶ **Finally . . .**
>
> You can now use the Paris métro: the whole system, not just those lines!
> If you have spare tickets you can use them on buses too; you may have to hand over two, three or four tickets for one journey.
>
> Now fill in your record sheet.

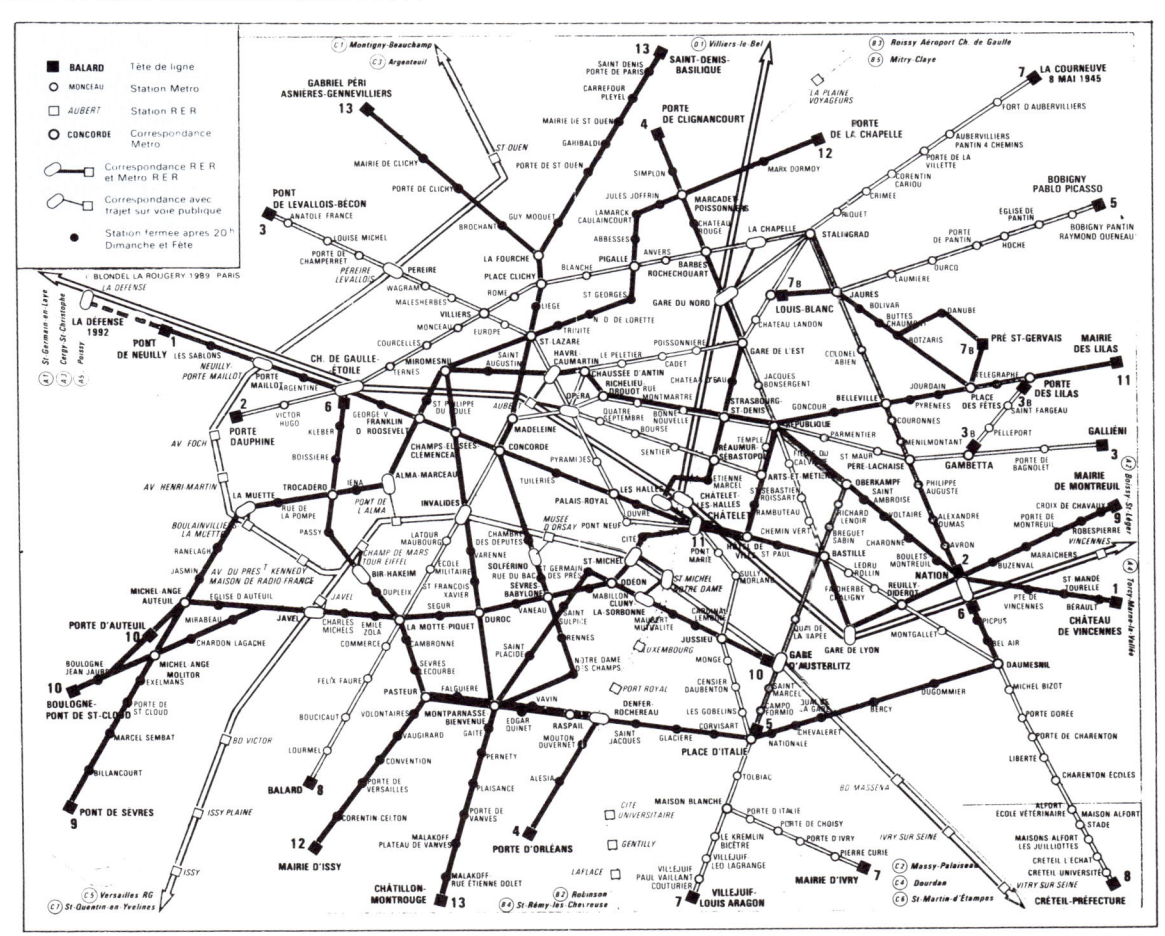

21 Feeling ill

Most people don't fall ill when they are abroad, but you must go prepared! Get an E111 form from the Post Office before you go, and show it when you see a doctor. Otherwise, you might have to pay for all your treatment, as France doesn't have the same system for National Health Service payments as the UK.
Take out holiday insurance as well.

▶ **Words you will need:**

au secours!	help!	ça fait mal ici	it hurts here
un médecin	a doctor	j'ai mal aux dents	I've got toothache
un/une dentiste	a dentist		
je suis malade	I'm ill	restez au lit	stay in bed
je suis blessé	I'm injured	ne mangez rien	don't eat anything
mon ami est malade	my friend is ill	buvez beaucoup d'eau	drink lots of water
mon ami est blessé	my friend is injured	voilà une ordonnance	here's a prescription
où est-ce que ça fait mal?	where does it hurt?		
vouz avez mal à la tête?	does your head hurt?		
vous avez mal à l'estomac?	does your stomach hurt?		
vous êtes blessé?	are you injured?		

Listening

A Look at the four questions, in the word list above, which you may hear.
Write in your book:

Where?   Head?
Stomach? Injured?

▶ Listen to these three conversations. Put a tick next to the words each time you hear those questions. ◀

B Write these words:

> Help
> Injured
> It hurts here
> Ill
> Toothache

▶ Listen to the conversations in A again. Put a tick next to each one, every time you hear those words. ◀

C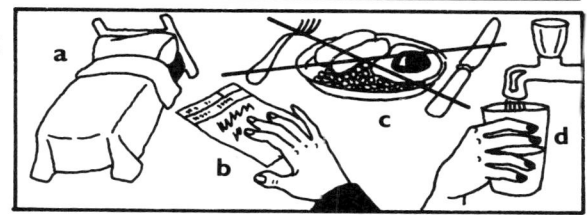

Write numbers **1 – 6** in your book.
▶ Listen to the doctor or dentist. Write the letter(s) of the instruction(s) she or he gives. ◀

Speaking

1 Au secours!
2 Un médecin! 
3 Un dentiste! 
4 Je suis malade! 
5 Je suis blessé! 
6 Ça fait mal ici. 
7 J'ai mal aux dents. 
8 Mon amie est blessée. 

A Look at the pictures above; say the captions to yourself.

Then work with a partner.

- Your partner points to the pictures, one by one. How quickly can you call out the right caption? Do them all, then swap over.

- Next, cover up all the captions. See if you can still say them to your partner. Do them in any order, and let your partner point to the right pictures to show that they understand. Then swap over.

B Call out what you would say in these situations.

1 You've just seen a road accident.
2 Your tooth hurts terribly.
3 You have a pain in your stomach.
4 You feel sick.
5 Your friend has tripped over and can't walk.
6 You think you've broken your leg.
7 You've got a pain in your chest.

C Work with a partner.

- You are feeling ill. Your partner asks you these questions:

- See if you can make up a conversation together.
- When you can do it without looking at the book, swap over – your partner is feeling ill.

Reading

A Your French colleague at work has gone home early.

- Read the note he left you.
- Then copy out the line below and fill in the gaps.

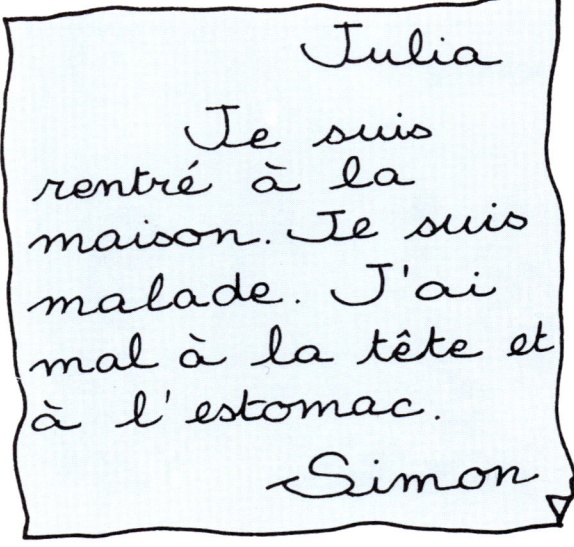

Simon is feeling ill. His . . . and his . . . hurt.

B Here is another note. Read it and then complete the sentence.

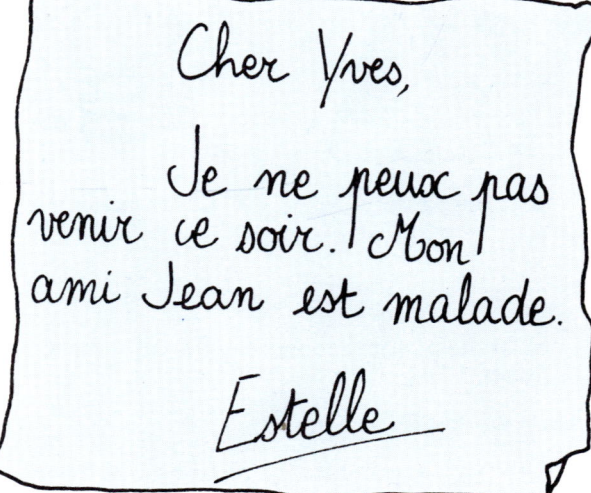

Estelle can't meet Yves this evening because . . .

C Read these two reports. Look for the words you are learning, don't be put off by the rest. Then answer the questions.

> Madame Lajambe est allée chez la dentiste. Elle avait mal aux dents.
> La dentiste a dit: 'Ne mangez rien!'

> Monsieur Aupied est allé chez le médecin.
> Il a dit: 'Bonjour, Docteur. Je suis malade. Ça me fait mal ici, à l'estomac.'
> Le médecin a dit: 'Restez au lit, et buvez beaucoup d'eau.'
> Il a donné une ordonnance à Monsieur Aupied.

1 Who went to the doctor?
2 Who went to see the dentist?
3 What was wrong with Madame Lajambe?
4 What was wrong with Monsieur Aupied?
5 What did the dentist say?
6 What two things did the doctor say?
7 Who was given a prescription?

Writing

A Copy these out, filling in the missing vowels:

1 J_ s_ _s m_l_d_
2 V_ _s _t_s bl_ss_?
3 _n m_d_c_n
4 V_ _l_ _n_ _rd_nn_nc_
5 _ _ s_c_ _rs!
6 B_v_z b_ _ _c_ _p d'_ _ _.

B You're going home to bed. Leave a note in French for your boss.
Say you have toothache and you feel ill.

> ▶ **To sum up . . .**
>
> You should now be able to get to a doctor or dentist, tell them what is wrong or what is hurting, and understand some of the questions they will ask you.
>
> If they give you a prescription, take it to a chemist – a *pharmacie* – Unit 34 will help you with that! You will have to pay, but you can claim the cost back through your E111 or your holiday insurance.
>
> Now fill in your record sheet.

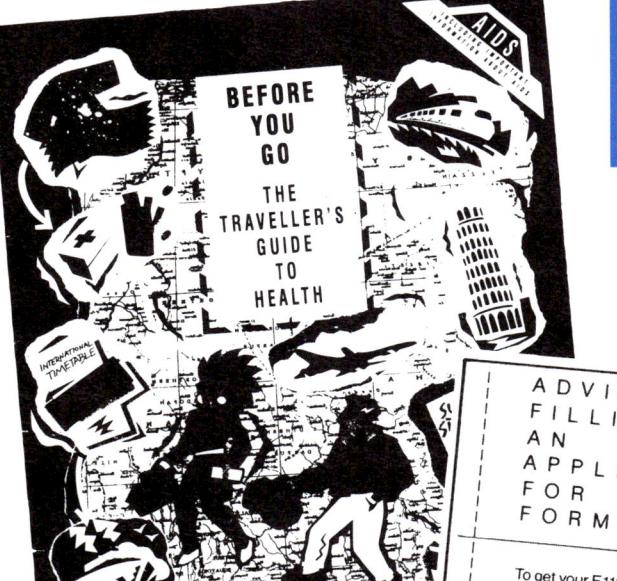

⦃22⦄ Dinner at a restaurant

▶ Words you will need:

1. *menu à prix fixe, 50 F* — fixed-price menu, 50 f
2. *salade de tomates* — tomato salad
3. *charcuterie* — mixed cold meats
4. *soupe à l'oignon* — onion soup

5. *rôti de bœuf* — roast beef
6. *côtelette de porc* — pork chop
7. *truite* — trout

8. *riz* — rice
9. *courgettes* — courgettes
10. *haricots verts* — green beans

11. *fromage* — cheese

12. *glace à la vanille* — vanilla ice cream
13. *mousse au chocolat* — chocolate mousse
14. *fruits* — fruit

15. *vin blanc* — white wine
16. *vin rouge* — red wine

17. *boisson comprise* — drink included
18. *service en sus* — service charge extra

19. *l'addition, s'il vous plaît* — the bill, please

In this fixed-price menu, you can choose a starter, a main course and vegetable, a sweet or cheese, and you get a quarter litre of red or white wine, all for 50 francs.

You should find water and baskets of fresh bread already on the table.

When you go in, you may need to ask the waitress or waiter for a table for the number in your party: *Une table pour trois, s'il vous plaît*, or *Une table pour cinq, s'il vous plaît*.

Listening

A Look at the pictures.

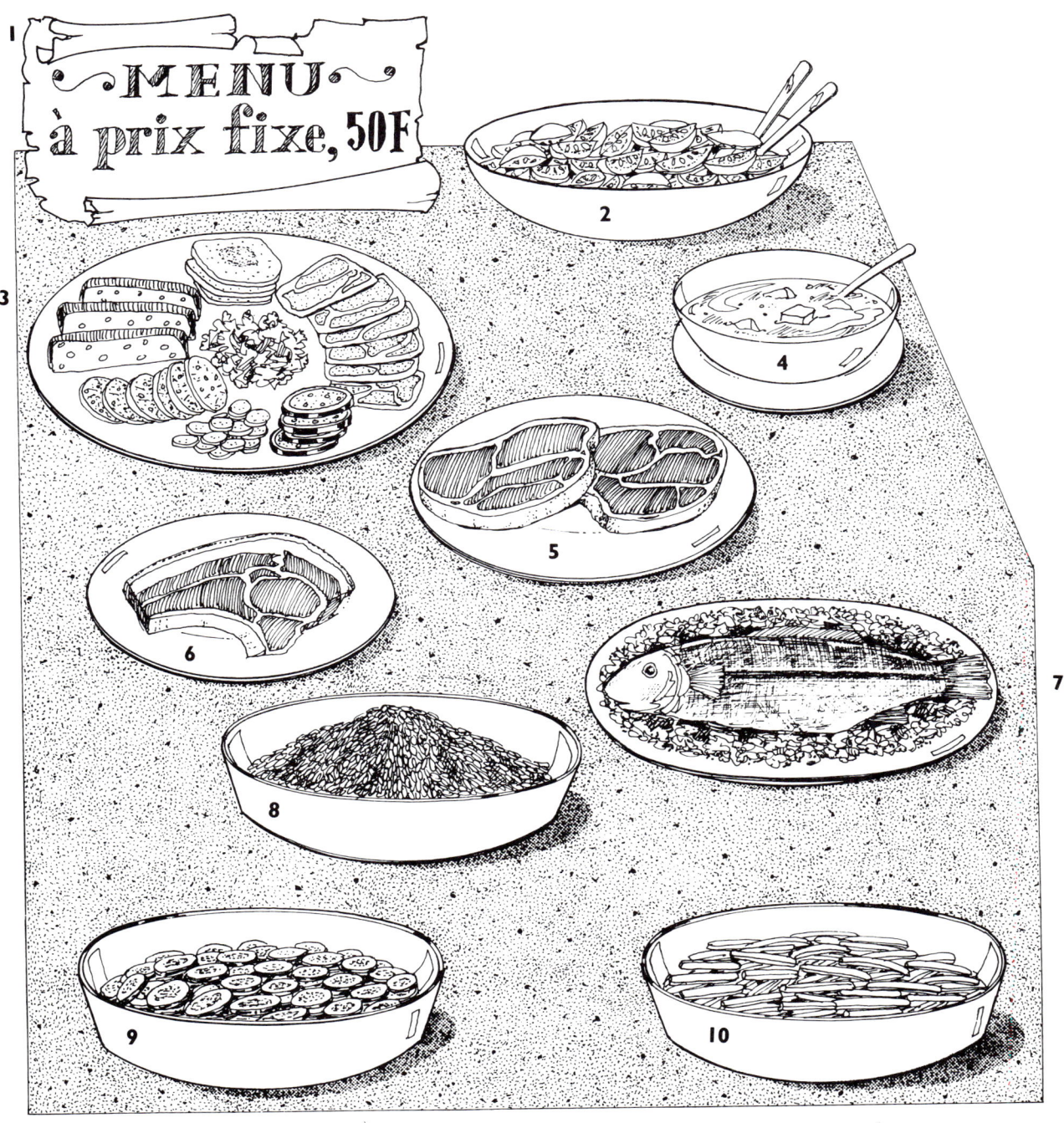

▶ You will hear people asking for those items on the tape. First, put **1 – 10** in your book. Then as you listen, put the correct number from the pictures to match what you hear. ◀

B ▶ This time you will hear people asking for dessert, wine or the bill. Put **1 – 7** in your book, look at the pictures, and put the correct number for each item you hear. ◀

C ▶ Now you will hear three people ordering a meal. They ask for the 50 F menu, then order five things from it. Write their names first: **Anne**, **Guy**, **Claire**. Then as you listen, write down the number of each item they ask for. ◀

Speaking

A Look at the pictures above and on page 87 and practise saying the names of the different items – use the menu to help you.

- Then practise asking for the 50 F menu
  – *Le menu à cinquante francs, s'il vous plaît.*
  and the bill – *L'addition, s'il vous plaît.*

- Then, see how many of the words you can say without looking at the menu, just from the pictures.

B Work with a partner and order a meal for yourself.

- Begin by asking for the 50 F menu: *Le menu à cinquante francs, s'il vous plaît.*

- Then look at the menu on page 86 and choose a starter, a main course with a vegetable, cheese or sweet, and some wine.

- Your partner points to the picture of each thing you order, to show that they understand.

- Then ask for the bill: *L'addition, s'il vous plaît.*

- Then swap over.

C Give your partner five numbers from the menu or the pictures.

- They have to order that meal, not forgetting to ask for the 50 F menu and the bill.

- Then they can give you five numbers to order.

Reading

A Copy these sentences into your book, either missing out or putting in the word 'not' to make sense.

1 A *menu prix fixe* is [not] a fixed-price menu.
2 *Le menu à 50 F* will [not] give you several courses for 50 francs.
3 *Service en sus* means service is [not] included.
4 *Boisson comprise* means a drink is [not] included in the menu price.
5 *L'addition* is [not] the menu.

B Look at these three bills.

1
```
Menu à 50F
Salade de tomates
Truite
Haricots verts
Fruits
Vin blanc
```

2
```
Menu à 50F
Charcuterie
Côtelette de porc
Courgettes
Fromage
Vin blanc
```

3
```
Menu à 50F
Soupe à l'oignon
Rôti de bœuf
Riz
Mousse au chocolat
Vin rouge
```

Answer these questions in your book by writing down the number of the correct bill.

a Who had roast beef?
b Who had cheese?
c Who had courgettes?
d Who had red wine?
e Who had the cold meat platter?
f Who had green beans?
g Who had soup?
h Who had fish?
i Who had chocolate mousse?
j Who do you think was on a diet?

Writing

A Make up two meals from the menu on page 86: one that you would most like, one that you would most dislike. List them in your book, in French.

B Write down in your book the French words for:

1 Drink included.
2 Fixed-price menu.
3 Service charge extra.
4 'The bill, please.'
5 Vanilla ice cream.

> ### ▶ And now...
>
> You should be able to order a meal. There will probably be a lot you don't understand on a menu, but you should know enough to get by. Some menus have the cheese as a separate course, so that you get some cheese and French bread before the dessert.
>
> It's worth looking for cheap restaurants that the French use, tucked away from the tourist traps.
>
> You will find another unit about restaurant meals in this book – Unit 4 – with a different menu.
>
> Now fill in your record sheet.

23 Filling in forms

If you have some sort of accident or emergency you will almost certainly have to give someone all your personal details. After a road accident you will have to fill them in on a *constat*, a report.

Or you may find yourself filling in a form at a hotel or a car hire firm.
You could also use this unit to help you if you applied for a job in France!

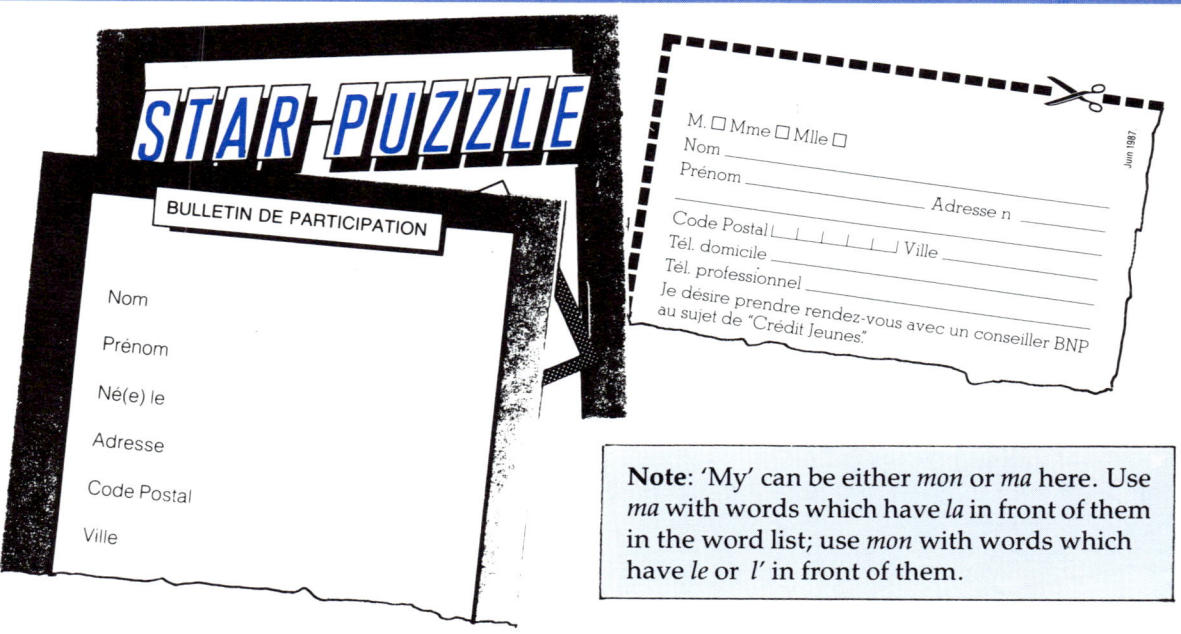

Note: 'My' can be either *mon* or *ma* here. Use *ma* with words which have *la* in front of them in the word list; use *mon* with words which have *le* or *l'* in front of them.

▶ **Words you will need:**

le prénom	first name	l'âge	age
le nom de famille	surname	la date de naissance	date of birth
l'adresse	address	la nationalité	nationality
l'adresse en France	address in France	britannique	British
la ville	town	c'est	(it) is
la rue	street	votre	your
le numéro de téléphone	telephone number	mon/ma	my

Listening

A When you are in an emergency, keep calm, and listen carefully.
▶ Listen to the five questions on the tape and match up the numbers with these: ◀

a first name
b surname
c address in France
d phone number
e age

B ▶ Now match the next five questions you hear with these: ◀

f nationality
g home address
h town
i street
j date of birth

C ▶ Listen to this conversation and pick out the five questions. They are all from **a – j**, as before. Write down the letters as you hear them. ◀

Speaking

A

Read the questions that the customs officer is asking.
Look how easy it is to make questions using *votre* and *s'il vous plaît?*

Read out the three questions and answers, with a partner. One of you is the customs officer, the other is the traveller. Then swap over.

B Work out and practise the questions you will have to ask in French to get this information from someone:

First name	:	Alexander
Surname	:	Wilson
Age	:	20
Date of birth	:	2 December 1969
Address in France	:	10 rue de Tivoli, Nîmes
Telephone number	:	22 22 23 15
Nationality	:	British

C Work with a partner.
- One of you asks the questions you've worked out in B.
- The other takes on the role of Alexander Wilson, and gives the answers. If you feel confident, give full answers:
  Mon adresse, c'est . . .
  If not, say just the one or two words you have to.

D Ask your partner for information about themselves: their own name, date of birth, nationality, and so on. Use the table below to help with your questions.
Then swap over. Practise until you can answer really quickly.

| Votre | nom de famille / prénom / adresse / âge / date de naissance / nationalité | s'il vous plaît? |

Reading

A Read this letter, and then copy and fill in details 1 – 6 on page 93.

> Monsieur/Madame
> J'aimerais travailler dans votre hôtel. Je me présente:
> Nom de famille: Marchant   Adresse: 34 rue du Soleil
> Prénom: Catherine   13000 Marseille
> Âge: 18   Numéro de téléphone: 23 34 74 60
> Date de naissance: le 2 novembre 1972   Nationalité: française

1 First name:
2 Surname:
3 Age and date of birth:
4 Telephone number:
5 Address:
6 Nationality:

B These French terms have a lot of extra letters. Decode them, then match them up with the details underneath.

1 rârgen
2 apirsénoim
3 adraltenisse
4 enartsionealisté

a britannique
b 17 ans
c 3, avenue du Pont
d Alan

C This form is taken from a leaflet about careers in the French army. People send the form in if they want further information.
Look at the personal details it asks for: then write down what you would put on the form if you wanted to send it in.

ARMÉE DE TERRE

Veuillez m'adresser une documentation complète sur les carrières et les métiers de l'Armée de Terre

Nom
_____
Prénom
_____
Age
_____
Adresse
_____
_____
Service National effectué   OUI   NON

Writing

A Unjumble these words:

MORÉNP   EADSSER   TÉNTAILIONA
LIVEL   MILELAF   UNROMÉ

B Imagine you want to apply for a summer job in a hotel in France. Write a letter: look back at Reading task A to help you.

Say you'd like to work there – *J'aimerais travailler dans votre hôtel* – and then use the words in this unit to give your personal details.

Names (first and surname)
Address (street and town)
Phone number, if any
Age and date of birth
Nationality

▶ **And finally . . .**

You should now be able to write down or tell someone who you are and where you live – whether you are applying for a job, being searched at customs or being taken into hospital.

Now fill in your record sheet.

24 Numbers and prices: 70–100

Unit 2 deals with numbers 1–69. You don't need to have done it to do this one, but it will be easier if you know numbers 1–20 at least.

Rather odd things happen to French numbers when you reach seventy. In English, it would go like this:

sixty-nine (69), sixty-ten (70), sixty and eleven (71), . . .
sixty-nineteen (79), four-twenties (80), four-twenty-one (81), four-twenty-two (82), . . . four-twenty-eleven (91), . . .

Here they are in French:

70 soixante-dix
71 soixante et onze
72 soixante-douze
73 soixante-treize
74 soixante-quatorze
75 soixante-quinze
76 soixante-seize
77 soixante-dix-sept
78 soixante-dix-huit
79 soixante-dix-neuf
80 quatre-vingts
81 quatre-vingt-un
82 quatre-vingt-deux
83 quatre-vingt-trois
84 quatre-vingt-quatre
85 quatre-vingt-cinq
86 quatre-vingt-six
87 quatre-vingt-sept
88 quatre-vingt-huit
89 quatre-vingt-neuf
90 quatre-vingt-dix
91 quatre-vingt-onze
92 quatre-vingt-douze
93 quatre-vingt-treize
94 quatre-vingt-quatorze
95 quatre-vingt-quinze
96 quatre-vingt-seize
97 quatre-vingt-dix-sept
98 quatre-vingt-dix-huit
99 quatre-vingt-dix-neuf
100 cent

CASSETTES VIDEO VHS SAMSUNG E 180
180 minutes
89 F
LE LOT DE 3

BARBECUE
10 kilos. FUN I E. convertible.
1 grille, 1 broche, 1 moteur, 1 plateau
85 F

Listening

A ▶ You will hear numbers between 70 and 79. Write them down in figures as you hear them. ◀

B ▶ Now you will hear numbers between 80 and 89. Just listen, and write them down in figures as you hear them. ◀

C ▶ Last of all, numbers 90 – 100. Write them down as before. ◀

D ▶ This time you will hear some prices. In each one, the first part is the number of francs, then you will hear the word *francs*, then the number of centimes.

Try to write down the whole price, for example 70, 80 F: but the francs are the most important, so concentrate on them. ◀

Speaking

A Practise counting from 70 – 100 by yourself, with the help of the word list and then without it, if you can.

B Work with a partner.
- Take it in turns to say a number in French; the other one listens and writes it down in figures. Do ten numbers each.
- Next, write down a number; can your partner say it? Again, do ten each.

C Work with your partner on prices.
- Write down a list of ten prices, in figures, for example 75, 80 F. Don't show them to your partner.
- Say them to your partner in French.
- Your partner has to listen and write them down.
- Then compare your lists – are they the same?
- Swap over – now it's your partner's turn to make a list of ten prices.

D **Numbers race!** Play in a large group divided into two teams, with one person to call out numbers.
- He or she calls out a number between 70 and 100 (or between 1 and 100).
- One person from each team writes it down quickly, on a blackboard.
- The first to write it correctly wins a point for their team.
- Keep score to see which team wins!

Or you can play in a group of three. One calls, the other two race to write down the figures on paper. Change parts after a while.

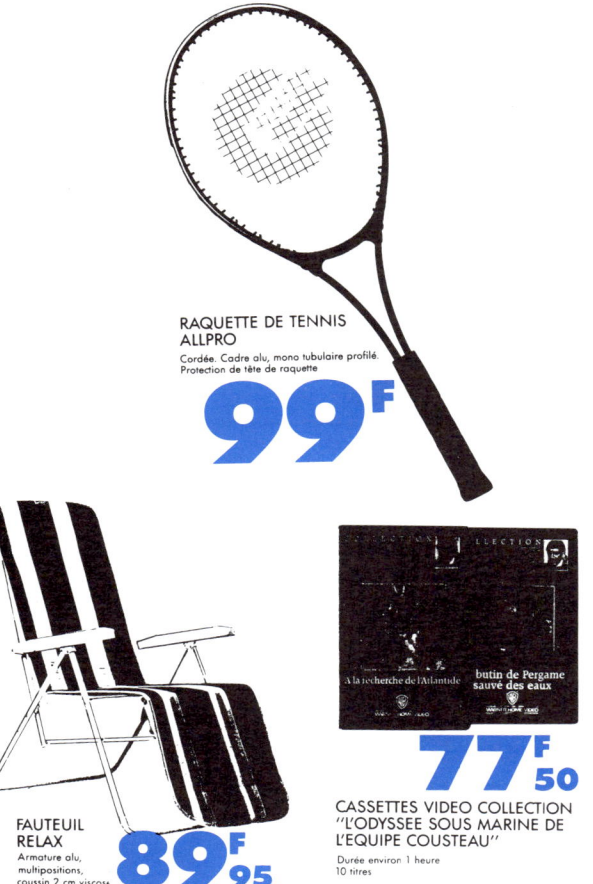

Reading

A

Answer these questions by putting the correct letter next to each number.

Which object costs:

1 cent francs?
2 soixante-dix francs?
3 quatre-vingts francs?
4 quatre-vingts francs soixante?
5 quatre-vingt-dix francs soixante-dix?
6 quatre-vingt-dix francs?
7 cent francs quatre-vingt-dix?
8 soixante-dix francs quatre-vingts?

B France is divided into regions called *départements*, each with a number as shown in the map below.
Here are five of them. Match them up with their numbers written out in words.
To start you off: **a** goes with **5**.

a 73 Savoie
b 75 Ville de Paris
c 80 Somme
d 88 Vosges
e 92 Hauts-de-Seine

1 quatre-vingts
2 soixante-quinze
3 quatre-vingt-douze
4 quatre-vingt-huit
5 soixante-treize

Writing

Choose ten numbers between 70 and 100 that you know. Write them down in words and figures.

> ### ▶ And finally . . .
>
> Don't worry about a price if you don't catch it all. Listen for the francs, and if there are some centimes mentioned after, add on another franc. Ten centimes are worth only about a penny. A franc varies in value, but at present it is helpful to think of it as about 10p.
>
> Now fill in your record sheet.

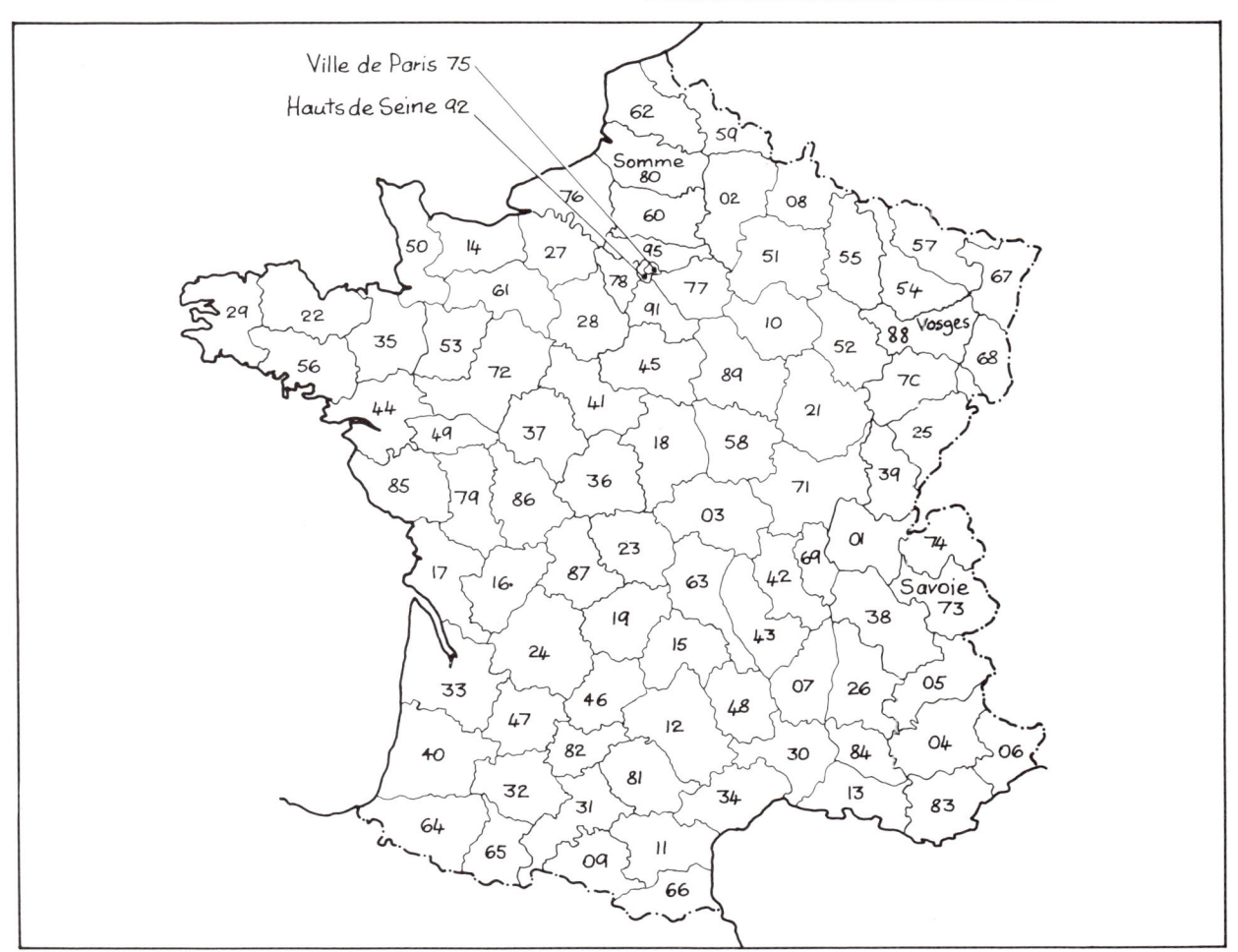

25 Directions

In this unit you will learn how to understand and give simple directions.

> **Words you will need:**
>
> | | | | |
> |---|---|---|---|
> | à gauche | left, on the left | la première rue | the first street |
> | à droite | right, on the right | la deuxième rue | the second street |
> | tout droit | straight on | la troisième rue | the third street |
> | continuez | go on, continue | | |
> | allez | go | au bout de la rue | at the end of the street |
> | tournez | turn | jusqu'aux feux | as far as the traffic lights |
> | prenez | take | | |

Listening

A The most important part of directions is 'left', 'right' or 'straight ahead'. Put numbers **1 – 8** in your book. ▶ Listen to the tape and for each one draw an arrow in the right direction. ◀

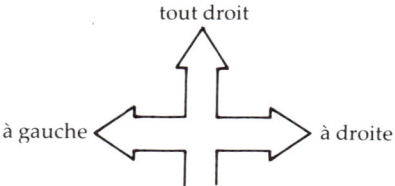

B ▶ Now listen carefully to that tape again, to hear the difference between *à droite* and *tout droit*. ◀

C Here's some more practice for left, right and straight ahead.

Write numbers **1 – 6**. Look at plans 1 – 6: you are standing at the X in each case.

▶ Listen carefully to the tape. Write down whether the directions you hear are true (**T**) or false (**F**). ◀

Be very careful when you start at the TOP or SIDE of a map!

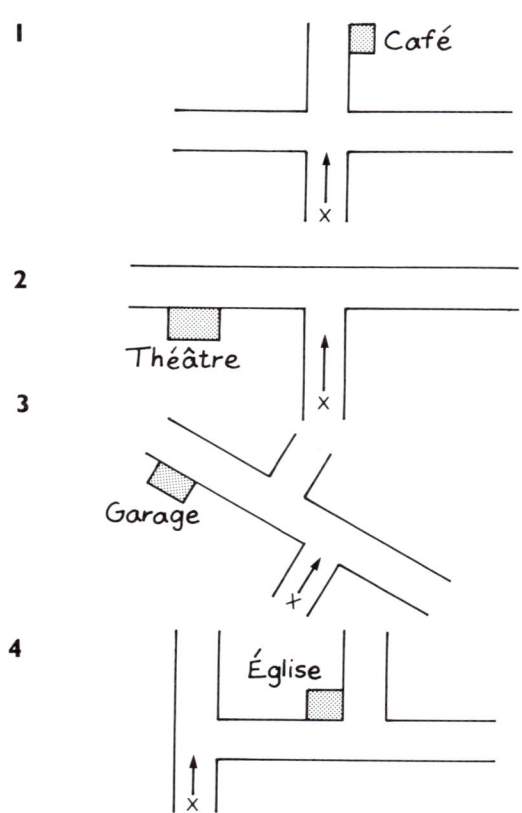

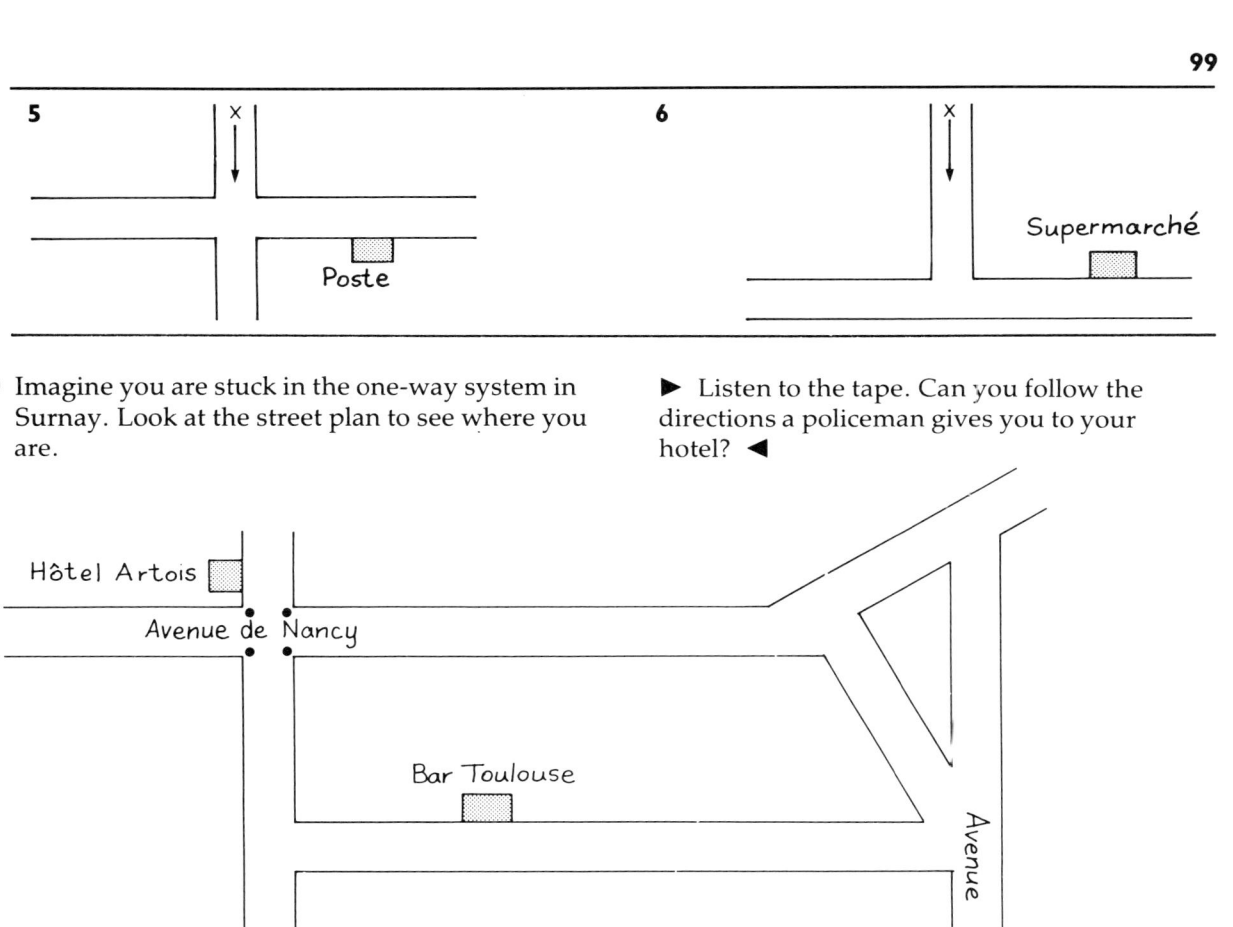

D Imagine you are stuck in the one-way system in Surnay. Look at the street plan to see where you are.

▶ Listen to the tape. Can you follow the directions a policeman gives you to your hotel? ◀

E The policeman did tell you more, but you've forgotten it! Find where you are now on the street plan.
▶ Listen to the directions a passer-by gives you. Can you follow them? ◀

Speaking

A

1 – On the right?
   – No, on the left.

2 – Take the third street on the left.

3 – Turn right.

4 – Go as far as the traffic lights.

5 – Is it at the end of the street?
   – Yes!

Learn these one by one.

Test yourself: how many can you say, looking only at the English sentences and not at the French?

B Use the street plan of Surnay on page 99. Work with a partner. Can you give these directions?

1 From the *Hôtel Artois* to the *Bar Toulouse*.
2 From the *Bar Toulouse* to the *poste*.
3 From the *poste* to the *camping*.
4 From the *camping* to the *supermarché*.
5 From the *supermarché* to the *poste*.

Reading

A Look at the signs. Which way must you go? Copy these signs and draw arrows to show.

1 **TOILETTES** tout droit	2 **RESTAURANT** à gauche
3 **TÉLÉPHONE** à droite	4 **TABAC** deuxième rue à droite

5 **FLEURS À VENDRE** première rue à gauche

B Look at the plan, read the directions below and write down where they lead you to. Each one starts off in a different place; the numbers on the map show you where.

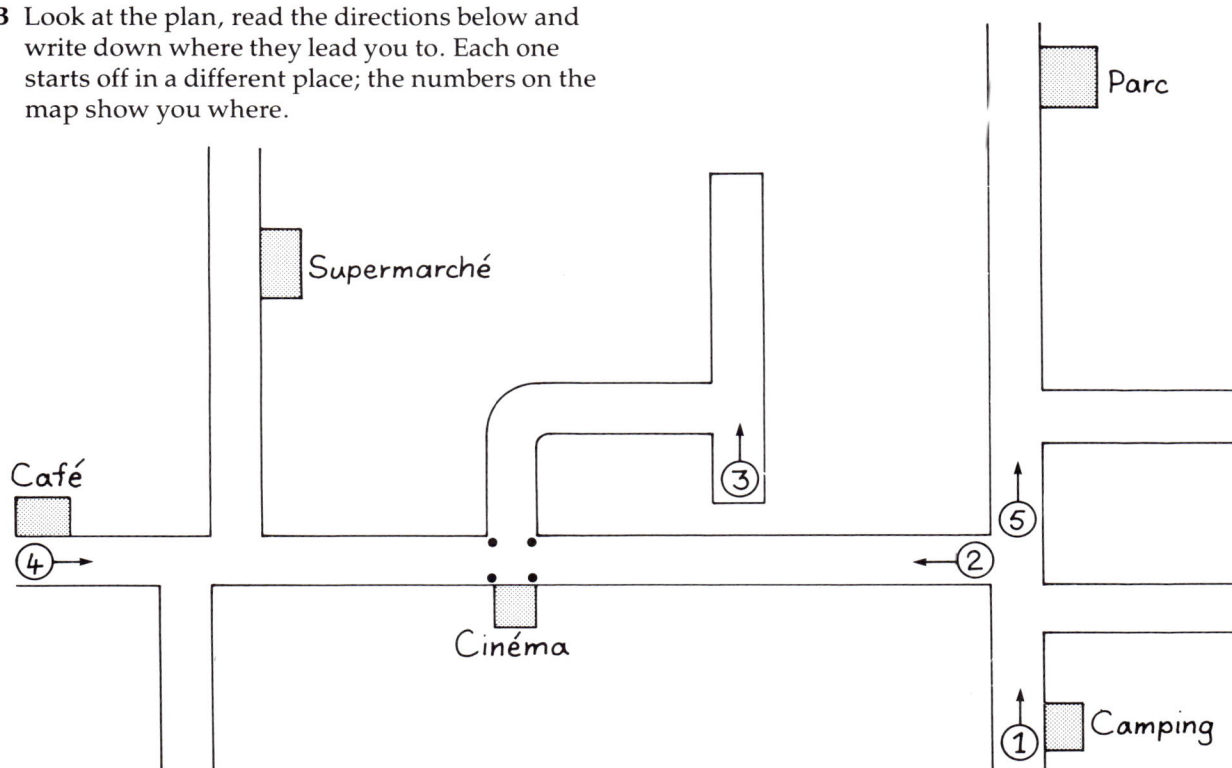

1 À gauche, puis tout droit.
2 Prenez la deuxième rue à droite.
3 Tournez à gauche, allez jusqu'aux feux.
4 Allez au bout de la rue, tournez à droite.
5 Continuez tout droit.

C A French friend of yours needs to get to the station. Write down some instructions to help her or him, using this information:

> Go straight on . . . as far as the traffic lights . . .
> Turn left . . .
> Take the third street on the right . . .
> It's at the end of the road.

Writing

A Unjumble these words used for giving directions. Write them correctly in French.

à guheca

outt rodit

à dtreoi

ecinoutzn

B Look at Speaking task B on page 100. Use the street plan of Surnay again, and write down in French the directions for journeys 1 – 5. Give as many details as you can.

> ▶ **And to sum up . . .**
>
> You should now be able to give simple directions and understand them when you have to ask the way somewhere. If you want more practice, use a real map, or make one up.
>
> Unit 9 deals with asking the way. If you have already done that unit, it might be useful to look back at it to remind yourself how to do that.
>
> Now fill in your record sheet.

26 Buying bread and cakes

French bread is wonderful, but must be bought and eaten fresh. Cakes may be expensive, but are made from top quality ingredients. *Boulangerie* over a shop means bread is sold: *Pâtisserie* is for cakes. Sometimes one shop has both names, indicating that they sell both. Supermarkets usually have counters selling bread and cakes, too.

▶ Words you will need:

une boulangerie	bread shop, bakery
une pâtisserie	cake shop
une baguette	bread – a French stick
une brioche	a bread roll, bun
un croissant	a croissant (a crescent-shaped breakfast pastry)
un pain au chocolat	a roll with chocolate filling
un gâteau	a cake
s'il vous plaît	please
merci	thank you
pièce	each, per slice
deux francs cinquante	two francs fifty centimes
un, deux, trois, quatre, cinq, six	1 2 3 4 5 6
comme ça	like that

You don't need to learn the names of all the cakes; just point with your finger and ask for *Deux gâteaux comme ça, s'il vous plaît.*

a BOULANGERIE
b PÂTISSERIE

c Baguettes 2,50 F

d Brioches 2,00 F pièce

e Croissants 3,00 F

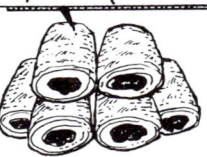
f Pains au chocolat 3,00 F pièce

g Gâteaux 5,00 F pièce

Listening

A Look at the picture on page 102. ▶ You will hear someone asking for some food or looking for a bread or cake shop. Just listen for the names. Put **1 – 7** in your book, and write the correct letter from the picture by each number. ◀

B ▶ This time they are asking for more than one. Put **1 – 5** in your book, and then put the number they want, and the letter of the item from the picture, in each case. For example, for the first one write **3 g.** ◀

C ▶ Now you will hear the prices too. Put **1 – 6** in your book, then write down in figures the prices you hear.
For example, *deux francs cinquante* – **2,50 F.** ◀

▶ Listen to that tape again. What are the people buying, and how many? Use the letters from the picture, and a number. ◀

D ▶ These people are asking for a mixture of things.

- Copy the grid
- Listen to the tape.
- Write how many they want, in the correct columns; so if they ask for *une baguette*, put a **1** in the first column. ◀

	c	d	e	f	g
1					
2					
3					
4					

Whether you can understand the price asked for depends on how many French numbers you know. Avoid the problem if need be; before you ask, work out how much it will be from the price tags, or read the total from the till.

Speaking

A Practise with the pictures on page 102 asking for one of each item. Don't forget to say *s'il vous plaît!*

- Then work with a partner, taking it in turns to ask for an item and to be the shopkeeper saying the price. Don't forget *merci* too!

B Next, ask your partner for more than one of each item, any number up to six. Say, for example, *Trois baguettes, s'il vous plaît.*

- The shopkeeper works out the total price and says it or writes it down.
- Then it's their turn to ask for something.

C Now try asking for a list of three different items: for example, *Un croissant, deux brioches et cinq pains au chocolat, s'il vous plaît.*

- Your partner will probably need to jot down a bill!
  For example,

  3 F + 4 F + 15 F = 22 F

- If this seems hard, first practise together what you are going to say, before acting it out.

If you have time, act out these situations using paper cut-outs of the items; then you can be sure that your partner knows what you are asking for, and how many.

Reading

A Here are some shop signs.

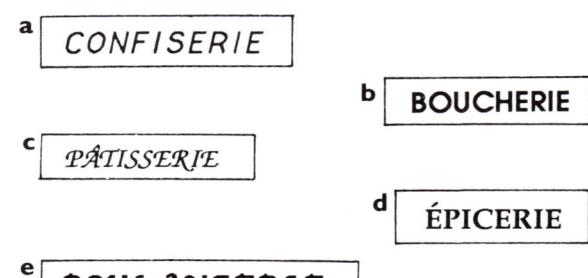

a CONFISERIE
b BOUCHERIE
c PÂTISSERIE
d ÉPICERIE
e BOULANGERIE
f CHARCUTERIE

1 Where would you go to buy bread?
2 Where would you go to buy cakes?
3 Where would you go to buy *baguettes*?
4 Where would you go to buy a strawberry tart?

B Look at these shopping lists.

Pierre

trois baguettes
un pain au chocolat
deux croissants

Antoine

quatre gâteaux
une baguette
six brioches

Cécile

un gâteau
deux pains au chocolat
cinq brioches

What is each person going to buy? Write down a number and a letter (from the picture on page 102) for each item on the lists.

C Look at the picture on page 102. Work out the prices for each of these:
1 1 French stick
2 3 bread rolls
3 2 cakes
4 3 croissants
5 2 chocolate rolls

D Work out a bill for each person in task B, using the prices in the pictures.

Writing

A You have some tomatoes, cheese and drinks.

Write out a shopping list, in French, from the picture, to complete your picnic lunch.

There are four of you.

B You have jam, butter and coffee.

Write out another shopping list, in French, from the picture, to complete your breakfast.

You need enough food for three.

C Unscramble these words and write them out correctly.

sstpâieire

eutgaâ

tsicrsano

tuteegab

ganreeilbuo

> ▶ **To sum up . . .**
>
> You should be able to buy bread and cakes without any trouble.
>
> A hint: the phrase *comme ça, s'il vous plaît* can be used in any shop, with a pointing finger and a number, if you don't know the words for what you want to buy.
>
> Fill in your record sheet now.

27 Accident or emergency

If you see an accident or a fire, or have something stolen, you need help quickly! This unit tells you what to say on the phone.

▶ **Words you will need:**

un téléphone	a telephone
au secours!	help!
au feu!	fire!
la police	the police
une ambulance	an ambulance
vite!	quickly!
c'est . . .	it's . . .
urgent	urgent
un accident	an accident
un vol	a theft
un incendie	a fire
quelqu'un est malade	someone is ill
quelqu'un est blessé	someone is injured
qu'est-ce qu'il y a?	what's the matter?
où êtes-vous?	where are you? (make sure you know where you are, before you are asked!)

a un téléphone

b la police

c une ambulance

Listening

A ▶ You will hear people asking for help. Write numbers **1–9** in your book. Then listen and write the letter from the pictures to match their problem. ◀

B ▶ Listen to that tape again for 'Help', 'Quickly' and 'It's urgent'. Write **H**, **Q** or **U** if you hear them. If the sentence has none of them, leave it blank. ◀

C ▶ Listen to these three phone conversations. Each time, the operator asks two or three questions. Here are some questions to choose from. Write **1–3**, and then write down the letters of the questions you hear. ◀

    a Is someone ill?
    b Where are you?
    c What's the matter?
    d Is anyone injured?

d Au feu! C'est un incendie

e C'est un accident

g Quelqu'un est malade

f C'est un vol

h Quelqu'un est blessé

Speaking

A

Can you say all three in a row? How urgent can you be?

B Look at the pictures on page 106–7.

- Practise saying the captions, until you can say them without looking at the words, only at the pictures.
- As it gets easier, add in *Au secours! Vite! C'est urgent!*
- Work with a partner: they point to the correct picture to show they understand.

Turn back to back with your partner. Say them again, but make sure they are loud and clear!

C Call out what you would say on the phone in these situations.

1 A motorbike has crashed into a lorry.
2 Your brother has broken his leg.
3 Someone has stolen your wallet.
4 Your hotel room is on fire.
5 You have just been mugged.

Reading

A Read the messages and answer the questions.

1

2

3

4

What happened . . .

1 at the Hôtel Maxi?
2 at the cinema?
3 at the Café Noir?
4 in room number 50?

B Read these extracts from Doctor Poulet's diary. Then copy and complete the sentences below.

septembre

3 lundi
accident au Collège Leman
3 élèves blessés

4 mardi
incendie à l'Hôtel Victor Hugo
2 enfants malades

5 mercredi
vol au Crédit Mutuel
2 employés blessés

At the Leman school:
1 There was an ....
2 Three pupils were ....

At the Victor Hugo hotel:
3 There was a ....
4 Two children were ....

At the Crédit Mutuel:
5 There was a ....
6 Two employees were ....

Writing

Write down how you would say in French:

1 Help!
2 It's urgent!
3 Police!
4 Fire!
5 An ambulance!
6 Hurry!

> ### ▶ To sum up...
>
> You should be able to ask for help – and shout if need be!
>
> Don't worry too much if you don't understand what the telephone operator says to you: make sure you have said what the problem is, and where exactly you are. Give your phone number if you think that will help.
>
> Of course, we hope you'll never need to use the language in this unit!
>
> Now fill in your record sheet.

28 Likes and dislikes

This unit is about liking and disliking activities and sports; you can use the same phrases to talk about liking people, pop stars, places, food . . .

▶ **Words you will need:**

j'aime . . .	I like . . .	le sport	sport
je n'aime pas . . .	I don't like . . .	le football	football
aimez-vous . . . ?	do you like . . . ?	la gymnastique	gymnastics
oui/non	yes/no	la télévision	television
		la musique	music
nager	swimming	les films	films
voyager	travelling	les boums	discos
lire	reading	les voitures	cars
		la mode	fashion, fashionable clothes

Listening

A ▶ You will hear some people talking about their likes and dislikes. All you have to do is decide if they are saying that they like (*j'aime*) or don't like (*je n'aime pas*) whatever it is. Put **1 – 6** in your book and listen to the tape. For each one, put a tick if they like it and a cross if they don't. ◀

B Look at the pictures. ▶ Then listen to the tape: you will hear people saying something about activities a – f. Put **1 – 6** in your book and then write the letter of the activity you hear. ◀

▶ Now for the other six activities in the pictures, g – l. Put **7 – 12** in your book and again, write a letter to match what you hear. ◀

a nager	**b** voyager	**c** lire	**d** le sport
e le football	**f** la gymnastique	**g** la télévision	**h** la musique
i les films	**j** les boums	**k** les voitures	**l** la mode

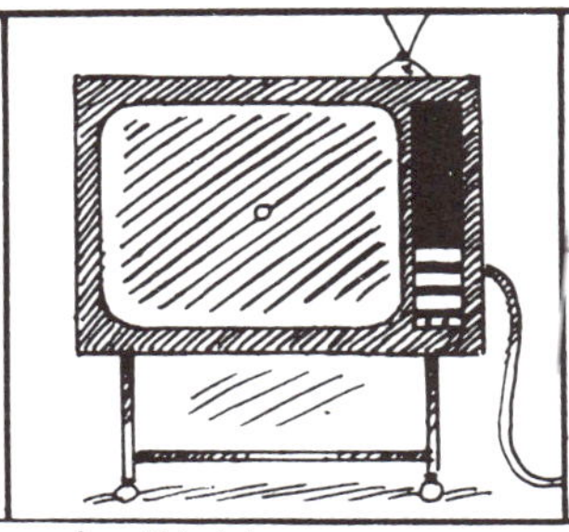

C ▶ You will hear people being asked if they like something. They will answer yes or no. Put **1 – 6** in your book. For each one, put a letter (**a – f**) to match the activity, and a tick or a cross for yes or no. ◀

▶ Six more people are being asked if they like something. Write numbers **7 – 12**, and then as before put a letter for the activity (**g – l**) and a tick or a cross. ◀

Speaking

A Look at the pictures of the activities on page 111.

- Say what they are, with or without the words covered up.
- Then say whether you like or dislike them. Start with *J'aime* . . . or *Je n'aime pas* . . . and put in the name of the activity.

B Work with a partner.

- Point to a picture and ask your partner *Aimez-vous* . . .? with the name of the activity.
- They reply *Oui, j'aime* . . . or *Non, je n'aime pas* . . . with the name of the activity.
- Then your partner chooses a picture and asks you.
- Go on until you have both asked and answered for all twelve pictures.

C What do I like? Play a guessing game, in pairs or in a larger group.

- One person acts out or mimes an activity they like from this unit.
- The other(s) have to guess what it is, by asking *Aimez-vous* . . .? with the name of the activity.

D Survey. Find out which TV programmes, singers, pop groups, and films your friends like.

- Ask them *Aimez-vous* . . .? and put in the name of something.
- They reply *Oui, j'aime* . . . or *Non, je n'aime pas* . . .
- Keep a score of the replies – you could make up a grid like this:

	Karen	Mike
Dallas	✓	✓
Tomorrow's World	✗	✓

or like this:

	aime	n'aime pas
The News	3	7
EastEnders	6	4

Reading

Read these descriptions from small ads, of people looking for new friends.

> Je m'appelle **Claire**.
> J'aime voyager, j'aime la mode et les films. Je n'aime pas le sport.

> Je m'appelle **Paul**.
> J'aime le sport, les boums et la musique. Je n'aime pas la télévision.

> Je m'appelle **Sophie**.
> J'aime les voitures, j'aime nager et lire. Je n'aime pas les boums.

> Je m'appelle **Yann**.
> J'aime la gymnastique, le football, et la télévision. Je n'aime pas lire.

Now answer these questions. Write the first letter of the person's name.

1. Who doesn't like TV?
2. Who likes music?
3. Who doesn't like reading?
4. Who does like reading?
5. Who likes fashion?
6. Who likes cars?
7. You like swimming, but not discos. Who is most like you?
8. You like gymnastics and football. Who is most like you?
9. You don't like sport, but you like to travel. Who is most like you?
10. You like music and discos. Who is most like you?

Writing

Write a small ad for yourself.

- Use the Reading task to help you.
- Start off with your name.
- Choose four activities from this unit – more if you can.
- Say whether you like them or dislike them.

> ▶ **To sum up . . .**
>
> This unit deals with some of the most common interests. The ruling passion of your life may not be here. If you go to France, it's worth learning how to say what you like doing best, to help you make friends.
>
> Now fill in your record sheet.

▶29◀ Making friends on holiday

This unit should get you started with making friends. You can talk about where you are staying, what it's like. You can even invite yourself to someone's home!

▶ **Words you will need:**

vous êtes . . . ?	you're staying . . . ?	*c'est où?*	where is it?
nous sommes . . .	we're staying . . .	*c'est à . . . kilomètres d'ici*	it's . . . kilometres away
dans . . .	in . . .		
un hôtel	a hotel	*c'est comment?*	what's it like?
un appartement	a flat	*formidable!*	great!
un camping	a campsite	*pas mal*	not bad
une auberge de jeunesse	a youth hostel	*affreux!*	awful!
un gîte	a (holiday) cottage	*on peut vous rendre visite?*	can I/we come and see you?
en ville	in the town		
à la campagne	in the country		

Listening

A

Write **1 – 9** in your book. ▶ Listen to the tape; you will hear some people talking about where they live or are on holiday. Look at the pictures above and write the correct letter(s) next to each number. ◀

B ▶ Listen to these two conversations. Then write the word(s) you need to complete the sentences. ◀

1 Madame Leclerc is staying in a . . . .
2 It is . . . kilometres away.
3 It is (great/OK/awful).
4 She (wants/does not want) visitors.

1 Monsieur Thomas is staying in a . . . .
2 It is in the (country/town).
3 It is . . . kilometre(s) away.
4 He thinks it is . . . .
5 He (wants/does not want) visitors.

Speaking

A

un gîte
un hôtel
une auberge de jeunesse
un appartement
un camping

- Can you say the names of these different types of holiday accommodation?
- Then cover up the words, and see if you can still say the names.

B Work with a partner. You have met on holiday and want to know **where** you are staying.

- One of you asks *Vous êtes où?*
- The other chooses a picture and replies *Nous sommes dans . . .* and finishes off the sentence.
- To show they've understood, the first one points to the right picture.
- Then swap over.

C Work with a partner again. Find out more about where you're staying: where it is, what it's like, whether you can visit.

- Do this one first of all: one asks the questions, the other answers:

C'est où?	C'est à 2 kilomètres d'ici
C'est comment?	C'est formidable!
On peut vous rendre visite?	Oui!

- Practise until you can cover up the words and say it looking at the three symbols.

- Then use this table. Take it in turns to ask the questions and give answers.

C'est où?	C'est comment?	On peut vous rendre visite?
2 km	😐	✗
1 km	🙂	✓
2 km	☹	✗
1 km	😐	✓
2 km	🙂	✓

D Make up a new conversation with your partner. Ask each other about your holiday accommodation: ask four questions each, using what you've practised in B and C.

Reading

A Wordsquare. Can you find twelve new words (of three or more letters) from this unit?

S	D	E	C	J	E	U	N	E	S	S	E
A	P	P	A	R	T	E	M	E	N	T	O
F	O	R	M	I	D	A	B	L	E	N	S
F	A	L	P	A	U	B	E	R	G	E	E
R	R	C	A	M	P	I	N	G	L	M	R
E	T	Î	G	A	R	B	R	O	M	M	E
U	N	E	N	L	E	T	Ô	H	U	O	S
X	A	V	E	L	L	I	V	U	T	C	T
S	E	R	T	È	M	O	L	I	K	S	Y

B Look at these newspaper adverts. Then complete the five sentences.

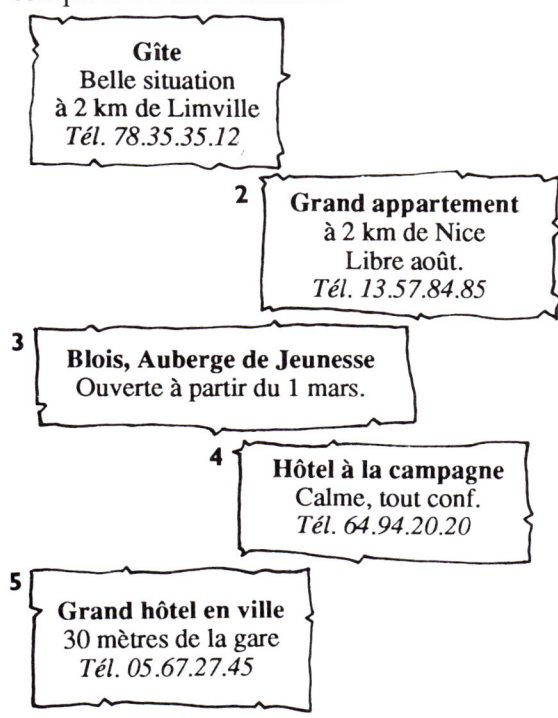

Can you find the right advert?

a The country hotel is advert number . . .
b The hotel in the town is advert number . . .
c The youth hostel is advert number . . .
d The holiday cottage is advert number . . .
e The holiday flat is advert number . . .

C Read this invitation someone has left you at your hotel reception.

> Nous sommes dans un gîte à la campagne.
> C'est à 5 kilomètres d'ici.
> C'est formidable!
> Venez nous rendre visite!
> Jeanne et Jean-Luc

Write down (in English) four things you can find out about where Jeanne and Jean-Luc are staying.

Writing

A Someone's been forgetting the French words! Copy this out, changing all the English words into French.

Salut! **We are staying** dans un **holiday cottage** à la **country.**

It's five kilometres d'ici. C'est **great! Can we** vous rendre visite?

B Find the nine French words in this line and write them out.

C Write notes to a friend, like the one you received in Reading task C.

1 Say you are staying in a flat in the town.
   It's three kilometres away.
   It's not bad.
   Ask if you can visit them.

2 Say you are staying in a hotel in the country.
   It's five kilometres away.
   It's awful!
   Ask if you can visit them.

▶ Summary

You should be able to find out a little about other holidaymakers now, and invite yourself to see them.

Think about what you have done in this unit then fill in your record sheet.

▶30◀ Buying fruit

You can buy fruit at supermarkets or grocers. Many French towns have markets, with stalls spread with fruit and vegetables of very high quality.

In this unit, you will learn how to buy the kind of fruit you might want as a snack or with a picnic lunch.

▶ **Words you will need:**

s'il vous plaît	please	pommes	apples
merci	thanks	fraises	strawberries
		pêches	peaches
un kilo de . . .	a kilogram of . . .	cerises	cherries
une livre de . . .	500g (a pound) of . . .	raisins	grapes
une demi-livre de . . .	250g (half a pound) of . . .	tomates	tomatoes

You can work out your total cost from the price tickets on display, to have your money ready. Look carefully – the price may be for a kilo or for a smaller amount.

a

POMMES 8,50F Kg

d

FRAISES 15,00F 500g

b

PÊCHES 12,50F Kg

e
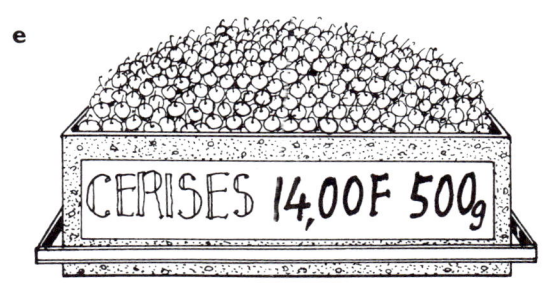
CERISES 14,00F 500g

c

TOMATES 8,00F Kg

f

RAISINS 16,00F Kg

Listening

A Put **1 – 6** in your book. ▶ Listen to these names of fruit; find each one in the picture above and put the correct letter by each number. ◀

B ▶ These people are ordering fruit. Listen for the amount they want.
If you hear *un kilo* . . ., put **kg**;
for *une livre* . . . put **500g**;
and for *une demi-livre* . . . put **250g**.

Put **1 – 6** in your book and listen to the tape. ◀

C ▶ Now listen to the same tape again. This time, see how much more you can understand.

- Listen for the **fruit** – write down the letters from the pictures.

- Listen for the **price** (1 – 15 francs) – put it in numbers. Sometimes, after the word *francs*, you will hear *cinquante* which means 50 centimes, so put 50 too. ◀

Here's the first one, to start you off:

1b 12,50 F

Speaking

A Can you say the types of fruit in French? Practise with the pictures on page 119, covering up the writing to test yourself.

Work with a partner: test each other on the names of fruit by pointing to a picture and seeing if they can say the name.

B Buy some fruit from your partner. (You can make this as easy or as hard as you like!)

- Use the pictures on page 119. Take it in turns to order; choose *un kilo*, *une livre* or *une demi-livre* of any fruit.
- Your partner, the shopkeeper, tells you the price in French. Work out the price from the pictures and say it or write the figures down; or make up a price of your own!
- Here are some examples:

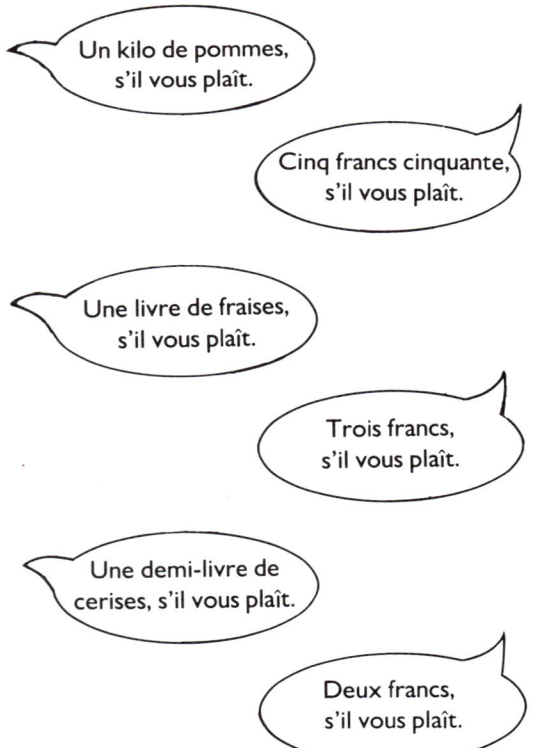

C Try ordering a list of things from the shopkeeper, who can jot down a bill for you. Take turns. Don't forget *s'il vous plaît* and *merci*.

Reading

A Here is a shopping list.

> un kilo de pêches
>
> un kilo de pommes
>
> une livre de fraises
>
> une livre de tomates
>
> une demi-livre de cerises
>
> une demi-livre de raisins

Write down in English what is going to be bought: the name of the fruit and the quantity.

B All you need to do this time is read prices and work out amounts. Write down in figures the cost of each of these, from the price tags in the pictures on page 119:

1. un kilo de pommes
2. une livre de raisins
3. une livre de tomates
4. une demi-livre de fraises
5. une livre de cerises
6. un kilo de pêches

Writing

A Make up your own shopping list in French, with four items on it – more if you can.
Include the amount you want – *une demi-livre de* . . ., *une livre de* . . . or *un kilo de* . . .

B Draw all six types of fruit, and label them in French.

▶ And now . . .

You can now buy and enjoy fruit! It's the best fast food there is, and there is almost sure to be a little park nearby, with chestnut trees, a fountain and wrought iron chairs, where you can sit to eat it.

Now fill in your record sheet.

◣31◢ When your car breaks down

If you drive a car in France, make sure you are properly insured, and have some sort of breakdown service available. Let's hope you have no problems, but this unit will help you manage if something does go wrong.

▶ **Words you will need:**

allô	hello (on the phone)	*où êtes-vous?*	where are you?
je suis en panne	I've broken down	*sur*	on
qu'est-ce qu'il y a?	what's wrong?	*l'autoroute*	the motorway
j'ai un pneu crevé	I've got a puncture	*la nationale*	main road, A road
le moteur ne marche pas	the engine won't go	*la départementale*	B road
les freins . . .	the brakes . . .	*près de*	near
les phares . . . ne marchent pas	the lights . . . won't work	*en direction de*	going towards
		attendez près de la voiture	wait near the car

If you're driving in France it's useful to know the system of road names.
Just as we have motorways, A roads and B roads, and call them 'M23', 'A5', 'B209', and so on, the roads in France are *autoroutes, (routes) nationales* and *départementales*, shortened to A, N and D. So the **A2** is an *autoroute* or motorway, the **N10** is a *nationale* or A road, and the **D105** is a *départementale* or B road.

Listening

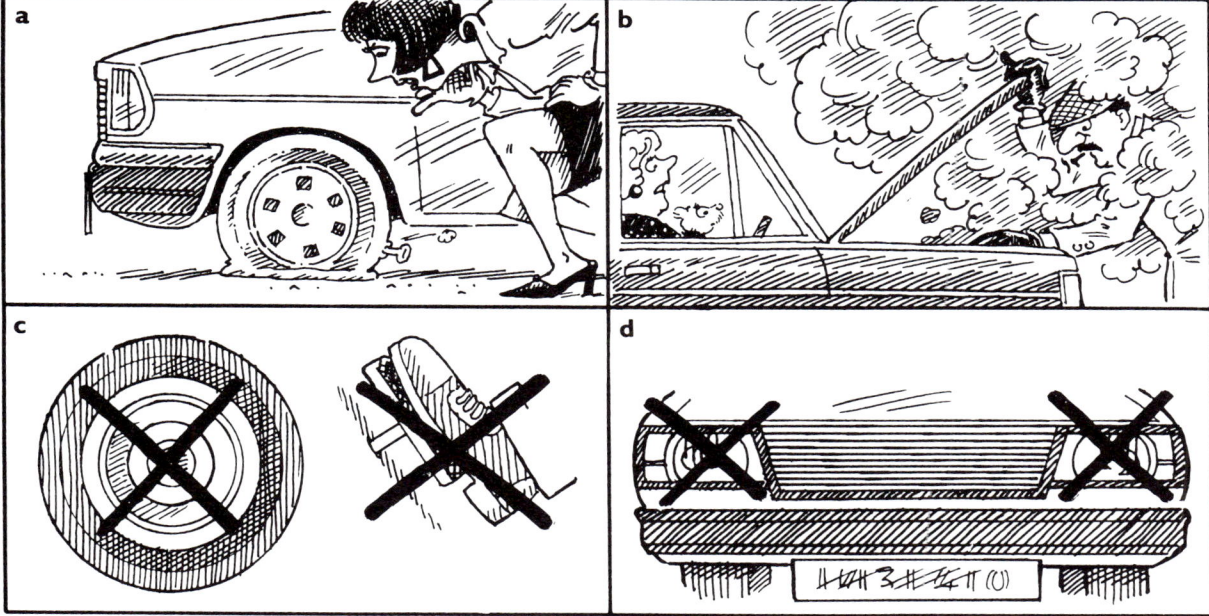

A ▶ Listen to these people reporting breakdowns. Write numbers **1–7**. Look at the pictures and put the correct letter next to each number. ◀

B ▶ Listen to these four conversations, and do the same again: what's wrong? ◀

C ▶ Write numbers **1–4**. Listen to that tape again to find out **where** they have broken down. You will hear the type of road: write **A** for *autoroute*, **N** for *nationale* and **D** for *départementale*. ◀

D ▶ These five people are saying the name of the town they are near or the direction they are travelling in. First, write down the names you will hear:

Cannes Marseille Bordeaux Annecy Lille

Then, as you listen, write **N** if the speaker is near the town, **D** if they are going in that direction. ◀

E Copy this table into your book. ▶ Then listen to the conversations and fill in any details you can. You may want to listen a few times to get them all. ◀

	What's wrong? (a, b, c, d)	Type of road (A, N, D)	Near ✓	Direction ✓	Told to wait near car? ✓
1					
2					
3					
4					

Speaking

A

J'ai un pneu crevé

Le moteur ne marche pas

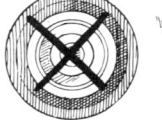

Les freins ne marchent pas

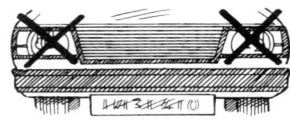
Les phares ne marchent pas

Can you say these? Cover up the French captions: can you still say the right thing?

Next, work with a partner. You've broken down in your car.

- Your partner asks *Qu'est-ce qu'il y a?*
- Choose one of the pictures and say what is wrong with your car.
- When you answer, they point at the picture to match what you're saying, to show that they understand.

B

Je suis sur l'autoroute

Je suis sur la nationale

Je suis sur la départementale

Can you say these without looking at the French?

Then work with a partner.

- They ask *Où êtes-vous?*
- Give answers; see if they can point to the correct picture.
- Then swap over.

C Practise this dialogue with a partner until you can do it without looking at the French words.

1 – I've broken down.
  – What's wrong?
2 – The engine doesn't work.
3 – Where are you?
  – On the motorway.
4 – Near Lille?
  – Yes, heading for Lille.
5 – Wait by the car.

Reading

A Look back at Speaking task C. Cover up the English captions and see if you can remember what the French means.

B Read this advert and then complete the sentences:

> Réparations de pneus, de freins et de phares
> **GARAGE NANCETTE**
> Nous sommes sur la N141 près de Cognac.

1 The garage is called ....
2 It is on an ... road.
3 It is near ....
4 It will mend ..., ... and ....

C A stranded motorist asks you to take a message to the garage in the next town. Read it and then answer the questions.

> Je suis en panne, sur la D30, près de Laval, en direction de Laval. Le moteur et les phares ne marchent pas. C'est une Citroën bleue. Envoyez un mécanicien, s'il vous plaît: j'attendrai près de la voiture.

1 What is wrong with the car?
2 Where is it exactly?
3 What sort of car is it, and what colour?
4 The note says 'Please ...'. What do you think the motorist is asking for?
5 What is she or he going to do now?

Writing

A Use the note in Reading task C to help you write a note for a garage. Give them this information:

You have broken down.
The brakes don't work.
You are on the main road – the N7 – near Menton, going towards Nice.
The car is a Renault.
You will wait near the car.

B Copy out these sentences and fill in the missing letters:

1 J_ s_ _s _n p_nn_.
2 _'ai u_ _ _eu _ _e_é.
3 L_s ph_r_s n_ m_rch_nt p_s.
4 _e_ f_ _ _ _s ne _ _ _ch_ _ _ _s.
5 L_ n_t_ _n_L.

> ▶ **To sum up ...**
>
> If you do break down, you should be able to get help by phone – or even by message.
>
> But do make sure your car is roadworthy before you leave! In fact, you must by law have with you a red warning triangle and spare bulbs for your lights.
>
> For full information about regulations in France, ask your travel agent, or contact the French Government Tourist Office (address on page 18, Unit 5).
>
> Now fill in your record sheet.

32 Taking notice

When in France, you will see lots of notices, some of which are helpful, some very important. This unit will help you recognise some of them.

It's worth remembering that if you see *Défense de . . .* or *Interdit*, it means that you are not allowed to do something!

a	OUVERT	open
b	FERMÉ	closed
c	SORTIE	exit
d	ENTRÉE	entrance
e	LIBRE-SERVICE	self-service
f	PÉAGE À 100 MÈTRES	toll point in 100m
g	CENTRE-VILLE	town centre
h	LA PLAGE	the beach
i	PRIORITÉ À DROITE	give way to traffic from the right
j	DÉFENSE DE FUMER	no smoking
k	DÉFENSE DE MARCHER SUR LES PELOUSES	keep off the grass
l	DÉFENSE DE STATIONNER	no parking
m	STATIONNEMENT INTERDIT	no parking
n	INTERDIT AUX PIÉTONS	no pedestrians
o	CAMPING INTERDIT	no camping
p	BAIGNADE INTERDITE	no bathing
q	INTERDIT AUX VÉLOS	no bikes
r	INTERDIT AUX VÉHICULES	no vehicles

Listening

A You won't often **hear** these, although a gendarme may shout one of them at you if you miss the notice!

▶ In this section, you are looking for signs from the first group, a – i. Put **1 – 9** in your book, listen to the tape, and put the correct letter for each one you hear. ◀

B ▶ Now for the second group of notices, j – r. Again, put **1 – 9** in your book, and put the correct letter by each number as you listen. ◀

Speaking, reading and writing

A Look at the pictures, first in one group and then the other. Read the French out loud. While you do that, see if you know what they mean, even with the English words covered up.

B Work with a partner.

Take turns to point to any sign from the pictures, covering up the English. Can your partner tell you what the sign means?

C Test your partner by saying the English words from any sign, and see if they can

a point to the right French sign, and
b say what is on it.

Score two points for both (a) and (b), one point for one of them. See who gets the most points.

D Answer these questions, working on your own. Put **1 – 10** in your book, and answer **yes** or **no**.

These are about the first group of signs.

1 The shop door says **FERMÉ**. Can you buy some bread now?

2 At a junction, it says **PRIORITÉ À DROITE**. Do you have right of way?

3 The petrol station says **LIBRE-SERVICE**. Do you wait for the attendant?

4 A sign points to **LA PLAGE**. Do you follow it if you want to go to the beach?

5 At the cinema, you see **ENTRÉE**. Is it the way in?

6 On the motorway, you see a **PÉAGE** sign. Do you get some money ready?

7 The supermarket door says **OUVERT À 9 h 30**. It's 9.00. Can you go in?

8 Driving through town, you see **CENTRE-VILLE**. Is it the way out of town?

9 In the métro, you see **SORTIE**. Do you follow it to get out?

10 You see **PÉAGE À 500 MÈTRES**. Do you have half a kilometre before you have to pay a toll?

E These questions are about the second group of signs. Answer with **yes** or **no**.

1. You see **INTERDIT AUX PIÉTONS**. Can you take your car there?
2. By the lake it says **BAIGNADE INTERDITE**. Is swimming allowed?
3. The waiting room says **DÉFENSE DE FUMER**. Should you smoke?
4. In the park, you see **DÉFENSE DE MARCHER SUR LES PELOUSES**. Can you sunbathe on the lawn?
5. In the street, you see **DÉFENSE DE STATIONNER**. Can you park your car?
6. In a field, you see **CAMPING INTERDIT**. Can you pitch your tent there?
7. On a narrow track, you see **INTERDIT AUX VÉHICULES**. Can you walk there?
8. You see **STATIONNEMENT INTERDIT**. Do you look for somewhere else to park your car?
9. Out cycling, you come to a **INTERDIT AUX VÉLOS** sign. Do you keep going?
10. You see a sign with **INTERDIT** or **DÉFENSE DE** . . . on it. Are you allowed to do whatever it is?

F Card game. Play this in groups of four.

- Get two sheets of paper, divide them into nine sections.
- Copy a different sign onto each section, so that you have 18 signs on 'cards'.
- Put them face down in one pile between you.
- Take turns to pick a card: if you can say what it means in English, keep it; if not, put it back at the bottom of the pile.
- When all the cards have gone, the player with most cards is the winner.

G Dominoes. Play this in groups of three or four.

- Cut sheets of paper into rectangles. You'll need enough rectangles for at least seven dominoes for each player.
- Draw a line dividing each rectangle into two sections.
- In one section, write a French sign, in the other, write the English for a different sign.
- Then play dominoes as usual; match up a French sign with its meaning in English.

H Answer these questions by writing out the correct sign or signs from the first group (a – i) on page 126.

1 What sign would tell you that the shop was shut?
2 Which sign would you follow for the beach?
3 Which sign would take you to the main shopping area of town?
4 Which sign would show you the way in at the swimming pool?
5 How would you know if a museum was open?
6 What sign would tell you that a motorway toll point was coming up in 300 metres?
7 You want to leave the motorway. What sign do you look for?
8 How do you know if a garage is self-service?
9 What sign would make you check carefully to the right, before driving off at a junction?

I Do the same with these, from the second group of signs (j – r).

1 Put your cigarette out if you see this sign.
2 Keep on the footpaths in the park if you see this sign.
3 You can't take your bike here.
4 Which two signs mean No Parking?
5 You can't walk here!
6 Find somewhere else to swim.
7 No cars, lorries or vans allowed on this road.
8 They don't want campers here.

> ▶ **And finally . . .**
>
> These are the most useful signs to know.
>
> Most road signs are international, so you will have no trouble with them.
> There may be signs about parking restrictions, such as zones where you display a disc showing your time of arrival – *Zone bleue: Disque obligatoire* – if in doubt, ask someone, or keep driving around for a free car park.
>
> Fill in your record sheet now.

33 Colours and sizes

You may want to buy some souvenirs to bring back – a T-shirt, for example; or you may want to buy some clothes while you are in France. This unit will help you talk about what you want.

▶ **Words you will need:**

un T-shirt	a T-shirt	bleu	blue
c'est combien?	how much is it?	blanc	white
c'est cher	it's expensive	noir	black
c'est trop cher	it's too expensive	grand	big
ce n'est pas cher	it's cheap	moyen	medium
		petit	small
rouge	red	long	long
rose	pink	large	wide
jaune	yellow		
vert	green	trop	too

Listening

A Write numbers **1–5** in your book. ▶ Listen to these people discussing prices. Are the prices high or low? Put an arrow pointing up – ↑ – if it's expensive, and an arrow pointing down – ↓ – if it's cheap. ◀

B ▶ These people are talking about the colour and cost of what they are buying. Write these colours in your book:

    RED

    PINK

    YELLOW

    GREEN

    BLUE

    WHITE

    BLACK

Listen to the tape. You will hear seven people; put the number of each one next to the right colour. ◀

C ▶ Listen to that tape again to hear the cost. First write numbers **1–7**. Draw an arrow going up – ↑ – for expensive, and down – ↓ – for cheap. (If neither is mentioned, leave it blank.) ◀

▶ Now for sizes. Write **1–5**. Look at the pictures, and choose the correct letter to match what you hear. ◀

E ▶ Listen to these four conversations. The customers don't want to buy the T-shirts. Find out what is wrong with each item. Write **1–4** and then for each one write '**Too** . . . .' and add the right word. ◀

F ▶ Listen to that tape again. Write down any other details – see if you can hear the price, colour or size. ◀

Speaking

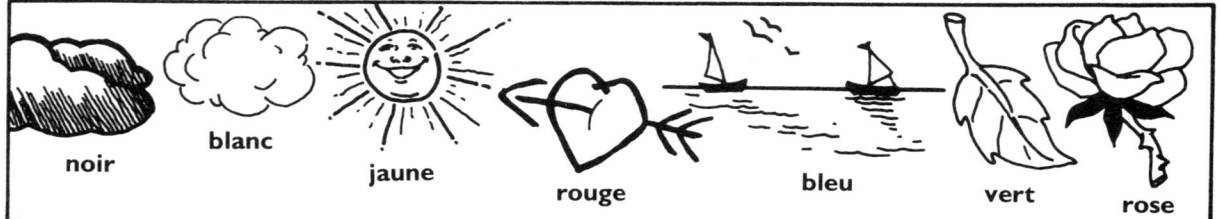

A Practise saying the sizes and colours until you can say them with the French names covered.

Work with a partner: say one of the colours or sizes and see if they can point to the right one to show they understand.

B Now ask for a T-shirt:

Un T-shirt, s'il vous plaît – un grand,
or *Un T-shirt, s'il vous plaît – un vert*.

Change the word on the end, to ask for different sizes and colours. Again, your partner has to point to the T-shirt of the right size, or to the picture of the right colour.

C

Can you say what is wrong with these T-shirts? For example, for the first one, say: *C'est trop grand*.

Say them to yourself first, and then work with your partner.

- Choose a picture.
- Your partner has to say what's wrong with that T-shirt.
- Then swap over; your partner chooses one for you to say.

D Work out a whole conversation together.

- You ask for a T-shirt.
- Your partner suggests a colour or size.
- You say there is something wrong with the size or with the price.

Reading

A

T-Shirts

**GRANDS PETITS
MOYENS LONGS LARGES**

■ *noirs et blancs,*
■ *rouges et roses,*
■ *verts et jaunes*

Look at the poster. Finish these sentences.

1 The shop is selling . . . .
2 They have these sizes: . . . .
3 Colours available are . . . .

B Read this extract from a letter and then complete the sentences.

et j'ai acheté trois T-shirts. Ils sont très à la mode, longs et larges. Et les couleurs? L'un est jaune et noir, les autres sont rouge et bleu, et vert et rose.

1 The style of the T-shirts is . . . and . . .
2 The first one is coloured . . . and . . .
3 The next one is coloured . . . and . . .
4 The last T-shirt is coloured . . . and . . .

Writing

A Look at the T-shirts on page 131 (Listening D). Write down the French word to describe the size of each one. The first one has been done for you:

   a. grand

B 'A green T-shirt' is *Un T-shirt vert*.

Write down the French words for:

   A red T-shirt
   A pink T-shirt
   A white T-shirt
   A black T-shirt
   A blue and yellow T-shirt

C 'It's too big' is *C'est trop grand*.

Write down the French for:

   It's too small
   It's too expensive
   It's too wide
   It's too long
   It's too big

▶ To sum up . . .

Whatever it is that you want to buy, you can now say what colour and size you want, or say what is wrong with what you have been offered.

Now fill in your record sheet.

34 At the chemist's

This unit will help you buy those essential things you either run out of or forget. The shop to look for is a *pharmacie*, or you might find them at a department store, supermarket, or campsite shop.

▶ Words you will need:

du dentifrice	toothpaste	*un déodorant*	deodorant
une brosse à dents	toothbrush	*des Kleenex*	paper tissues
du shampooing	shampoo	*des rasoirs jetables*	disposable razors
du savon	soap		
de l'aspirine	aspirins	*un peigne*	a comb
de la crème solaire	suntan cream	*une pharmacie avez-vous . . . ?*	chemist's have you got . . . ?
de la crème antiseptique	antiseptic cream		
des pansements	band-aids, plasters	*s'il vous plaît*	please

Listening

a du dentifrice
b une brosse à dents
c du shampooing
d du savon
e de l'aspirine
f de la crème solaire
g de la crème antiseptique
h des pansements
i un déodorant
j des Kleenex
k des rasoirs jetables
l un peigne

A ▶ Listen and try to identify what these are. Put **1 – 6** in your book, and put the correct letter from pictures **a – f** for each one. ◀

B ▶ Here are six more items. Write **1 – 6** and do the same again, using pictures **g – l**. ◀

C ▶ You will hear four people asking for something. Either they ask if the chemist has the item – *Avez-vous . . .?* – or they say the name and add 'please' – *. . . s'il vous plaît*.

First write **1 – 4**. Then listen carefully, and if you hear *Avez-vous . . .?* put a question mark (**?**); if you hear *s'il vous plaît*, write **P** for 'Please'. ◀

D ▶ This time, try to find out what they are asking for, and also how they are asking. Put **1 – 8** in your book. Then put either **?** or **P** as before, and the correct letter as well, next to each number. ◀

E ▶ These people are asking for three things each. Put **1 – 5** in your book, then listen and put the correct letters after each number. ◀

Speaking

A Use the pictures on page 135 to practise naming the items.
Say them to yourself. Cover up the French words and say them looking only at the pictures.

B **A card game**

- Cut or tear a sheet of paper into eight sections and draw eight items from page 135, one on each section.
- Get together with two or three other people.
- Put all your cards on the desk in one pile, face down.
- Take turns to pick a card. If you can name it in French, keep it; if you can't, put it back at the bottom of the pile.
- When all the cards have gone, see who has the most.

C Work with a partner. Ask your partner for something from the chemist's, using either *Avez-vous . . .?* or *. . . s'il vous plaît*.

- If you have cards from the last game, your partner can give you the correct picture.
- If not, your partner can point to the correct picture on page 135 to show they understand.

- Then swap over.
- When you can do that, try asking for more than one item at a time.

Reading

A Here are some labels you might see on counters in a supermarket or a large chemist's.

a **PHARMACIE**

b **DENTIFRICE**

c **SHAMPOOING**

d **SAVON**

e **BROSSES À DENTS**

f **CRÈMES SOLAIRES**

g **DÉODORANTS**

Answer these questions with the letter from the right label.

1 You want to avoid sunburn. What do you look for?
2 You've run out of deodorant. Where do you go?
3 You need some things from a chemist's, which sign?
4 You forgot your toothbrush. Where do you go?
5 You need to wash your hair. What do you look for?
6 You've lost the soap. Where could you buy some more?
7 You need some toothpaste. Which sign?

B Look at these shopping lists.

Alain

pansements
Kleenex
peigne
crème antiseptique

Claire

aspirine
crème solaire
dentifrice
savon

Marc

rasoirs jetables
brosse à dents
déodorant
shampooing

1 Who might have cut themselves?
2 Who might have a headache?
3 Who needs to shave?
4 Who needs to wash their hair?
5 Who wants soap?
6 Who needs a toothbrush?
7 Who needs a comb?
8 Who wants tissues?

Writing

A You are going on holiday. Write a list, in French, from this unit, of things you need to pack for everyday needs.

B You are putting together a simple first aid box for your car. Make a list, in French, of some things you need, from this unit.

> ### ▶ And finally...
>
> If you have special needs, such as for contact lens solution or special medicines, look the words up in a dictionary before you go to France.
>
> Now fill in your record sheet.

⟩35⟩ Arranging a meeting

You might want to meet a new friend for a drink, plan a night out on the town or arrange a day trip. For that you need to be able to discuss when and where to meet.

▶ **Words you will need:**

rendez-vous . . .	let's meet . . .
quand?	when?
où?	where?
ça va?	is that OK?
lundi	Monday
mardi	Tuesday
mercredi	Wednesday
jeudi	Thursday
vendredi	Friday
samedi	Saturday
dimanche	Sunday
le matin	in the morning
l'après-midi	in the afternoon
le soir	in the evening
à mon hôtel	at my hotel
au bar	at the bar
au restaurant	at the restaurant
chez moi	at my home
chez vous	at your home
chez Marc	at Marc's house
ici	here

Listening

A ▶ Listen to these seven people suggesting **which day** they should meet. First write down the seven days of the week in English, then write the numbers next to the correct days as you hear them. ◀

B ▶ What **time of day** will they meet? Listen to find out if it is morning, afternoon or evening. Write **AM** for morning, **PM** for afternoon, and **EVE** for evening. There are five to listen to. ◀

C ▶ Listen to these people to find out **where** they will meet. Write numbers **1 – 8** in your book. As you listen, write the correct letter from the pictures below, next to the numbers. ◀

(Be careful with *chez moi* and *chez vous*: these can easily get mixed up!)

D Copy this table into your book:

	Day?	Time of day?	Where?
1			
2			
3			
4			
5			

▶ Listen to the whole of each of these conversations, and then fill in as much information as you can. ◀

Write short answers, and for 'Where?' use the letters from the pictures above. So for number 1, for example, you could write:

    MON   PM   a

Speaking

A Look at the page from the diary. Work with a partner. Suggest meeting on different days, like this:

> Rendez-vous lundi? Ça va?

Your partner can say *'Oui, ça va'* or be awkward and suggest another day:

> Non! Rendez-vous jeudi!

Keep going until you can say it easily and think you know all the days of the week.

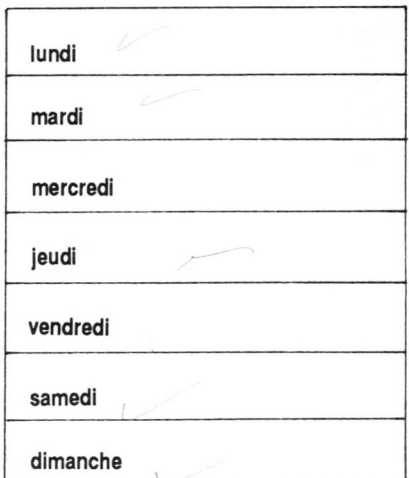

B When you can do Task A, suggest what time of day as well. You just need a day of the week and a time – two words only – like this:

> Lundi soir?   Oui, ça va.

Or be difficult and answer:

> Non! Lundi après-midi!

C Now arrange where you are to meet.

- Take turns to suggest one of these places; the other points at the right picture to show they understand.
- Then, choose a picture; your partner has to suggest meeting there. Try this with the French words covered up, looking only at the pictures.

D Now put it all together: try and arrange to meet your partner at these times and places:

	Day	Time	Place
1	Monday	morning	hotel
2	Friday	evening	bar
3	Sunday	afternoon	here
4	Wednesday	evening	restaurant
5	Saturday	afternoon	at your home

E When you can do Task D easily, see **how long** you can take to agree on everything. Keep asking *Où?* and *Quand?* and saying *Non!*

Reading

A Read these notes, then copy and complete the sentences below.

1 Maxine! Rendez-vous à mon hôtel dimanche matin? Christine

2 Éric! Rendez-vous samedi, chez moi? Le soir? Pierre

3 François! Rendez-vous au bar, jeudi? L'après-midi? Frédéric

4 Joël! Rendez-vous chez vous, mardi soir? Céline

a Christine wants to meet Maxine on . . . day AM/PM/EVE at . . . .
b Éric and Pierre are going to meet at . . . .'s home on . . . day.
c Frédéric will be in the bar on . . . day in the AM/PM/EVE.
d Céline wants to meet at . . . .'s home on Tuesday AM/PM/EVE.

B Which two days of the week can you NOT find in this line?

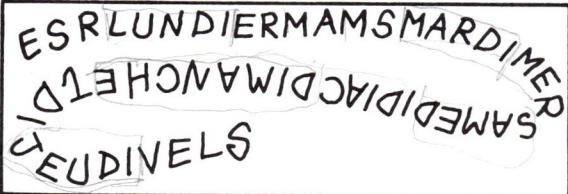

C

VISITE de la VILLE — dimanche matin ici

MUSÉE OUVERT — mardi et mercredi, l'après-midi

Look at the posters and answer the questions.

1 When is the tour of the city?
2 Where do you have to meet for it?
3 On which days is the museum open?
4 What time of day is it open?

Writing

A Can you write down all the days of the week without looking at them?
Here are the first letters, to get you started:

l _ _ _   v _ _ _ _ _ _
m _ _ _ _   s _ _ _ _ _
m _ _ _ _ _ _ d _ _ _ _ _ _
j _ _ _ _

B Write notes to these four people to arrange where and when you are going to meet them. Use the information here and look at the notes in Reading task A to help you.

1 Maxine! – at the bar – Wednesday – afternoon
2 Éric! – at the restaurant – Tuesday – evening
3 François! – at your home – Friday – morning
4 Joël! – at my home – Sunday – afternoon

> ### ▶ To sum up . . .
>
> You should now be able to arrange to meet someone, and also to understand posters or tourist information telling you when some event is to take place.
>
> Think about what you have done in this unit, then fill in your record sheet.

Acknowledgements

Design: Raynor Design

Illustrations: David Till, Jean de Lemos, Debbie Clark, Julia Osorno, Ian Foulis

Photographs: Marie Fleith, David Simpson/MGP, Frédéric Pitchal/MGP, Keith Gibson, Lorraine Sennett, Peter Waygood, Colorific

We are grateful to the following for allowing us to reproduce published material: Europcar UK Ltd. (page 58), Edward Briscoe Design/Avis (page 58), Pariscope (page 70), RATP (page 81), Crown copyright with the permission of the Controller of Her Majesty's Stationery Office (page 85), Gîtes Ruraux de France (page 114), Ligue Française pour les Auberges de la Jeunesse (page 114), Les Palatines, Résidence de Tourisme (page 114).

Every effort has been made to trace all the copyright holders but the publishers will be pleased to make the necessary arrangements at the first opportunity if there are any omissions.

© Mary Glasgow Publications
First published 1990
Reprinted 1990 (twice), 1991 (twice), 1992, 1993, 1994, 1995

ISBN 1-85234-285-4

Mary Glasgow Publications
An imprint of Stanley Thornes (Publishers) Ltd
Ellenborough House, Wellington Street
Cheltenham GL50 1YD

Typeset in Linotron Palatino with Gill Sans
by Northern Phototypesetting Co. Ltd., Bolton.
Printed and bound in Great Britain
at T.J. Press (Padstow) Ltd, Cornwall.